Introduction

Silicon Valley is a vision, a state of mind, a dream. It is the Gold Rush incarnate, the 21st century field of dreams for millions of entrepreneurs around the world who toil and save in order to come here so they can dig deeply into the rich soils of this sacred technology field to strike their fortunes. The media trumpets the success of Silicon Valley companies like Google and Facebook, so when people find out I grew up in the valley and am a serial entrepreneur, they eagerly ask: What was it like back then? Did you meet Steve Jobs and Steve Wozniak? Has your company gone public? How do I raise venture capital? Should I move to Silicon Valley? How do we create a Silicon Valley in our region?

Silicon Valley has been exhaustively studied and analyzed by journalists, academics, business writers, and policymakers alike. So much has been written about this mythical place that one wonders if anything new can be told. But having grown up in the valley, I know there are thousands of untold stories and more being experienced everyday. Instead of writing another business book analyzing Silicon Valley, I thought it would be more interesting to tell my personal stories, straight and unvarnished, about growing up and working in the valley, just the way it happened. I want to take you along with me so you know how if felt to grow up in the valley and work with some of the top business managers and entrepreneurs who regularly gambled their money, reputations and efforts to create new ventures or do tough corporate turnarounds.

This book is mostly about successful people and companies. It is a celebration of the valley, not a business school case study. Most startups in Silicon Valley fail, which is why the valley is called "the valley of failures," but even here business failure is a well-kept secret. My friends and colleagues who fail usually tell me that they're "moving on." We both smile, knowing they tried, learned some hard lessons, and will try something new again, hoping to invent the "Next New Thing." It is this optimism, this willingness to take risks and, most importantly, this ability to bounce back from failure that distinguishes Silicon Valley from most places around the world, where failure ends careers. In the valley, we live and breathe entrepreneurialism; it's in the air and our blood.

My memories of Silicon Valley are very different from most journalistic and academic accounts I've read, which are usually written from a "West Valley" perspective. Silicon Valley is divided into two very different regions. "West Valley" is the wealthy, white and now Asian suburbs where almost everyone goes to college and has a nice job; it is what you read about in most Silicon Valley books. It features Stanford University, Fred Terman, Schockley Semiconductor, Intel, National, Apple, Google, Facebook, and all the other Silicon Valley giants. Rarely told is the "East Valley" and San Jose, which is heavily populated by working-class ethnic groups who toil as unsung line engineers, janitors, secretaries, shopkeepers, and delivery people. These are the people I grew up with who provide the gritty foundation for Silicon Valley's rise to fame and glory. They are more like John Steinbeck's Joad family, not Leland Stanford's heirs.

My experience straddles both valleys. I grew up in schools in downtown San Jose, where most of my classmates were Mexican Americans, African Americans, Asian Americans, immigrants, and a tiny minority of others (i.e. Caucasians), but had the good fortune to study at Yale and Harvard's Graduate School of Design and work for a short while at Stanford's electrical engineering department, so I have lived and worked with the poorest and richest people in Silicon Valley. These worlds are poles apart, very much like Manhattan and Harlem, so my dual existence gave me a unique, stereo view of Silicon Valley. Even today, I feel like I'm crossing a culture warp between the rich, fast, prestigious West Valley and the slower, ethnic San Jose. My East Valley friends often ask what it's like to live and work with the elite they read about, but my West Valley friends rarely ask about the East Valley, except to acknowledge the Tech Museum downtown. So I have often served as a cultural and social interpreter between West Valley and East Valley, between Japan and the United States, and recently between Europe and the valley. I feel like a country bumpkin, which San Franciscans affectionately called us when I was a child, who has through a stroke of luck and a lot of hard work been given an E ticket ride in the heart of Silicon Valley. It has been an unforgettable journey so far and I am grateful to have had the opportunity to work with so many brilliant, warm, and generous people, from working-class families to the very elite. You're my friends and colleagues who have shown me that Silicon Valley is not just about technology and money; it's about imagining, caring, and living life to the fullest.

What I've always appreciated about Silicon Valley is its meritocracy and pragmatism. Unlike the East Coast, Japan or Europe, where pedigree is everything, in Silicon Valley on-the-job performance is paramount. What skills do you have? What can you do for us right now? How can you help us build our company? In the valley, we look for smart, creative, honest people with focus, drive and perseverance, not trust fund babies, educated loafers or corporate drones. The valley still has a thick glass ceiling; few women or minorities have risen to executive positions or sit on corporate boards, according to a recent study, but that is changing as the "old boys" realize Silicon Valley's future lies in global consumer markets and are hiring people to reflect this new, multi-polar world.

The Silicon Valley has faced many setbacks since its rise in the 1960s, yet bounced back stronger than ever. Like the Japanese daruma doll, it is designed to bounce back fast. The next wave of innovation will be no different, only bigger, faster and more global. But to understand the soul of Silicon Valley, you need to know its past, hopes, dreams and quirks. Hopefully, my personal stories will give you a better understanding of this magical place that lives and breathes for the future.

Alan Kay, formerly of Apple Computer and a Disney Fellow, best expresses the spirit of Silicon Valley: "The best way to predict the future is to invent it."

Welcome to Silicon Valley and enjoy the ride!

Sheridan Tatsuno

www.dreamscapeglobal.com,
http://siliconvalleyglobalnetwork.wordpress.com/

1950s-1960s: The Dawn of Silicon Valley

The Valley of the Heart's Delight

The year is 1955. A brilliant blue sky stretches over San Francisco Bay like an azure tent. My father drives our tan Ford station wagon down Highway 101, a lonely four-lane road with stoplights every ten miles, returning home after a busy workday in San Francisco. We look south to the Mount Hamilton range in the distance, shimmering green in the late afternoon sun. The air is fresh and clear. Only the solitary buzz of a Cessna breaks the silence of our sleepy valley. We pass Moffitt Field airbase, a Navy airport with occasional reconnaissance planes taking off past the huge, silvery dirigible hangar sitting on the mudflats like a beached whale. Rows of prune, peach and apricot trees line the lonely highway as we approach San Jose, which is surrounded by oceans of vegetable fields stretching into the distance. We are ecstatic heading toward one of the richest farmlands in America, Japanese Americans who had been released from World War II detention camps isolated in deserts, making our way back into American society. The "Valley of the Heart's Delight" was our new home away from the cold, foggy days of San Francisco, far from the nightmare of barbed wire fences, gun towers and tarpaper barracks of the war. I still remember the feeling of freedom and expansiveness as we breathed in the perfumed air of blossoms on our way home. To my parents, both devout Christians, this was the Promised Land. We were home. We had finally found our place in the world.

Do you know the way to San Jose? Twenty years later, Dionne Warwick's heartfelt song would lift the hearts of us country bumpkins in San Jose who yearned for dignity and respect. We were the sons and daughters of farmers, farm workers, cannery workers and shopkeepers – Italians, Mexicans, Japanese, Chinese, Blacks, Filipinos, Portuguese – who grew up downtown in simple worker homes down the street from the elegant Victorians of bankers, lawyers and doctors lining avenues of maple trees. We didn't have much money, just enough to live simply and happily during the 1950s in our small stucco homes. Life was simpler and calmer then, with few cars in the streets so we kids could play and ride bicycles without fear of getting hit or kidnapped. Neighbors would smile and take the time to chat and help each other. People walked around town since the streets were so quiet and safe.

On weekdays, the whistles of the fruit-packing canneries on Tenth Street would signal a new day. Thousands of workers would clock in, surrounded by a bustle of forklifts carrying pallets of canned fruits to waiting trucks lining the street. The air was filled with the pungent odor of drying fruit. I would ride by on my bicycle, watching fathers and songs, mothers and daughters, mostly Mexican and Filipino, climb into their rickety cars after a long day at work, smiling and sighing, glad to end another hard day at work. Sometimes we would get free samples from school friends whose parents worked in the canneries. During summer, we lucky ones got good-paying jobs there, slaving away at lid stamping lines from sunrise to sundown or, for brave souls who wanted higher pay, from sundown to sunrise. San Jose was a working-class town, a small farm town at the heart of one of the prettiest valleys in the world, filled with big Catholic families whose kids sat next to me in school. Ramirez, Gonzalez, Martinez, Tatsuno, Montoya, Alvarez – Tatsuno? Is your mother Mexican? The rounded shoulders of the Mount Hamilton range, topped by the silvery dome of Lick Observatory, lorded over us on clear days as we played baseball in the dusty field surrounded by canneries and warehouses. We were proud of our town, kings of the playing fields, and enjoyed weekends catching frogs in the Guadalupe River, riding bikes to Alum Rock Park, taking Sunday afternoon drives through orchards of blossoming fruit trees, and snitching fresh apricots in the summer. Life was good in our little paradise, our Valley of the Heart's Delight, as it was called then, and we thought it would never end.

But end it would. Across town, the rumblings of the electronics revolution were emerging around a little startup called Shockley Transistor. Totally unnoticed by most valley residents, this band of engineers would totally transform our lives within a decade. We did not know it then, but we "country bumpkins" from San Jose sat at ground zero of one of the most amazing industrial revolutions in history, one that still continues to amaze me. We would be transformed into Silicon Valley pioneers.

San Jose Airport

San Jose Airport was a quiet airstrip on the outskirts of town with a short Quonset hut for a terminal, a few hangars and parking spots for the silvery DC-3s that flew into town. The airport was so undeveloped that passengers had to carry their suitcases out to the tarmac, rainy or windy days, where bag handlers would then load them onto the plane. Then the DC-3 would lift off and bump along in the air currents over the foothills for the 90-minute flight to Los Angeles. Every spring, we would take the Blossom Time Tour of the valley, where the D-3C would circle blooming fruit trees spread out below like carpets of pink, yellow, and blue. It was truly the Valley of the Heart's Delight, a small, quiet valley with spectacular views of San Francisco Bay to the north, the Mount Hamilton range to the east, and the coastal foothills and Monterey Bay to the southwest.

In 1958, my father Dave Tatsuno, owner of <u>Nichi Bei Bussan</u>, a small shop in <u>San Jose's Japantown</u>, was appointed by City Manager Ron James to join the San Jose Airport Commission since he flew so much for the YMCA attending board meetings. My father consented and, in his typically diligent way, studied the airport plans since the question of expanding the airport had been raised. My father argued that San Jose should build an international airport since San Jose was growing, but a Lockheed manager said: "I work in aerospace and I can tell you one thing. San Jose will never need an international airport because there is no reason for anyone to come here." My father disagreed, saying families were moving in and someday San Jose would become a major metropolis. His comments elicited chuckles among the commission members seated around the conference table.

The airport commission's decision on a small expansion program would cost the valley dearly. Shockley Transistor spun out Fairchild Semiconductor, which spun out Intel, AMD, and National Semiconductor. President John Kennedy's clarion call to send a man to the moon triggered the space race with the Soviet Union, along with a nuclear arms race of Mutually Assured Destruction, creating thousands of engineering jobs. Kennedy's response to the attack on U.S. carriers in the Gulf of Tonkin off Vietnam and President Lyndon's expansion of the Vietnam War then boosted Pentagon spending at Lockheed, FMC Corporation and hundreds of other technology companies in Silicon Valley. Tens of thousands of engineers swarmed our little paradise like gold miners seeking their fortunes. Soon, aerospace labs, semiconductor factories, suburban housing, freeways and shopping malls covered our pristine farmland. Many of my poorer high school classmates were drafted and sent to Vietnam, while many of us lucky college students joined anti-war protests. By the time Neil Armstrong stepped onto the moon in 1969, San Jose had doubled in size to 200,000. The lonely country roads and fruit orchards where we played quickly vanished, forcing us to go further out into the country to find open space.

The moon landing was a mixed blessing since massive NASA layoffs forced nearly a third of all valley engineers into unemployment lines, but fortunately many found jobs at the new chip companies sprouting up in the orchards. So many tech companies popped up every month that tech journalist Don C. Hoefler coined the term "Silicon Valley" in his Microelectronic News newsletter to describe this new industrial cluster. By 1974, San Jose and its surrounding farmlands were paved over with tilt-up electronics companies, freeways, suburb housing and malls, despite the oil shock-induced recession. And although the San Jose Airport Commission kept expanding its undersized airport, it was always a step behind the valley's skyrocketing growth.

My father often shook his head with disappointment over the lack of vision that still plagues the valley today when one looks around at the traffic jams, strip malls, and lack of affordable housing for high-tech and support workers.

Never let the present limit your vision. Think beyond the immediate. Observe the world around you and visualize the many possible futures coming. You may be surprised by their speed, size and impacts.

Stanford Research Park

In 1960, my father and I were invited to visit the
Stanford University campus by our dear friend Kay
Tamaribuchi, who had graduated from MIT and
enrolled in Stanford's PhD program in chemistry. My
father, a UC Berkeley graduate, welcomed the chance to
visit the "Big Game" rival since he had other Nisei
friends who had studied there, but still it felt like walking
into foreign territory, far removed from the canneries
and small shops of San Jose. I recall being awed by
Hoover Tower, the Spanish architecture, the long
shadowed corridors, and the Memorial Church. It
seemed like a Spanish university dropped into the midst
of orchards and Eichler tract homes.

After touring the campus, Kay invited us to see the new
Stanford Research Park, where researchers were allowed
to pursue individual projects and launch companies. As
we drove up the lonely road out of town into the hills
covered with yellow grass and Spanish oak trees, I
wondered why Stanford put a research park in the
middle of nowhere.

We got out of the car and gazed around the virtually
empty orchard. From the hilltops, you could see the
entire Bay Area from San Francisco and Hayward to
south San Jose and the Mount Hamilton range, a very
impressive view. The bay was still undeveloped along
the eastern shore. Looking around, Kay pointed out

three small buildings sitting forlorn and alone in a grove of fruit trees. "This is the Stanford Research Park", he exclaimed proudly, as if it were the center of the research world. We looked carefully, but only saw some lonely shacks. My father, sitting on the San Jose Airport Commission, nodded with agreement, but I thought to myself: "Total flop. Nobody will ever come here." Indeed, at the time, it made absolutely no sense. Why would top researchers leave the comfortable intellectual environment of the East Coast, where most corporate labs were clustered, to come to the orchards of Stanford, a finishing school for rich kids, and work in these little shacks? I still remember that people laughed at us country bumpkins in San Jose and Palo Alto. We lacked the social graces and intellectual firepower of San Francisco, Chicago, New York, Boston and Washington D.C. We were just rural wannabes who lived simply, knew our neighbors, and minded our own business. We had no chance competing against the top universities and corporate labs on the East Coast.

As we left the research park, I remember feeling a mixture of disdain and puzzlement. Stanford Research Park trying to become a top research center? A noble, quixotic dream that was a long way from becoming reality – if ever. At best, it might develop advanced farming technologies since we all knew that the future of San Jose was automated farms. We had the best farmland and weather so we would be the most automated farmers in the world.

Never be trapped by the present. Sometimes, crazy visions of the future turn out to be much bigger than you can possibly imagine.

The Apollo Project

One of the joys of growing up in the 1960s was the Apollo Project. Launched with great fanfare by President Kennedy's inspiring speech, many of us young people dreamed of becoming astronauts who would someday circle the earth and walk on the moon. We would be Flash Gordon made real. It was a New Frontier; anything was possible. Despite a Cold War and racial tensions, we felt America was at the dawn of a great new adventure. It was an era of enthusiasm, joy and hope. If we could dream it, we could achieve it. We just had to buckle down, study hard, and work hard to realize our dreams.

So it was with great joy that I launched into a semester-long science project assigned by my elementary school teacher. We could explore anything we wanted. Of course, I chose the Apollo Project because I had been closely following it since Kennedy's speech. Going to the school library, I dug into popular and science magazines for articles about the project, coming up with an odd assortment of clippings, graphics and descriptions. One article provided a graphic of the Apollo plans for earth orbit, trajectory to the moon, moon orbits and landing trajectory, which I used to organize my paper. Then, with meticulous research and writing worthy of a NASA mission planner, I described the preparation, launch, and voyage of the Apollo space capsule in detail, by the hour, each task that the crew would perform. I imagined myself in the capsule orbiting the moon, descending to the moon in the lunar vehicle, landing on the dusty surface, hopping around on the moon while looking at the distant blue earth, blasting off, reuniting with the orbiting vehicle, heading back to earth, then entering a fiery tunnel and landing on the ocean. I was so deeply engrossed in this project, more than any project I had ever done before or since, that it still remains an intimate part of me. I was a NASA astronaut in training then and a Mars explorer now. Like many young Americans, I was caught up in the excitement and romance of space exploration.

While scuba diving with my father in Monterey Bay, I imagined myself an astronaut training to work in a weightless state. Standing on the sandy bottom, looking up at the schools of fish in the cathedrals of kelp and seeing the faint glimmer of the sun, I imagined looking back at earth. My father and I were aquanauts, two men on the moon like the images we saw in Life magazine. We had been inspired to scuba dive by Jacques Cousteau's "The Silent World" and in my mind I had entered the magical world of NASA space flights. Deep sea and deep space -- a heady mixture indeed for a teenager! When my father and I emerged from the depths to the sandy shore of Cannery Row, we would be greeted by dozens of curious families who had never seen scuba divers before since we were the only divers around.

I imagined being an astronaut greeted on 5th Avenue by admiring crowds. We were heroic adventurers.

To my delight, I received an A+ for my paper and proudly kept it in my files, privately following NASA's activities during the bitter anti-war protests and searing civil rights marches of the 1960s. Despite the ugliness and tension of American politics and the growing public distrust of science because of its use to develop napalm and nuclear bombs, the Apollo Project remained a bright spot. It was America at its best and I held it close to my heart and mind. As I followed NASA launches of Mercury and Gemini vehicles into space, I cheered and appreciated the hard work of the many Silicon Valley engineers who were working at NASA Ames and its systems suppliers. They were our local heroes, an antidote to growing public revulsion to science and technology. They gave us inspiration and hope.

So it was with utter shock and delight when I learned that the moon landing was scheduled for July 20th -- my birthday! It was as though NASA had rewarded my diligence by choosing my special day. Returning home from Yale to work in a strawberry cannery in San Jose that summer, I remember my glee and anticipation as the Apollo rocket lifted off the launch pad at Kennedy Space Center and soared into the blue sky. America's hopes soared skyward with the Apollo crew. Emotionally, I was seated with them in the capsule. I felt like a child again, enthralled by space flight. Then I remembered: my science class report! Rifling through my bookshelf, I found it, old and dusty, as I had written it, to religiously follow the mission, and found its content still valid. I knew every phase and step of the mission by heart. It was my space Bible, my journey to the stars. We sat glued to the television and radio. As the lunar module approached the moon, I followed the mission, step by step, while listening to the frequent updates on the status of the mission -- the earth orbits, the trajectory to the moon, the moon orbits, and the final descent to the surface of the moon. I was Mission Control, reporting to my family and friends on the status of the mission.

On July 20th, my family and I sat in total awe during the final moments as the lunar module descended to the moon. We held our breaths, fearing something would go wrong, especially when Armstrong could not find a clear landing spot and almost had to abort the landing, then gripped ourselves in steely silence when Houston signaled the go-ahead sign, waiting for the capsule to descend. We watched as the moon surface filled the screen with splotchy black and white shadows, then waited in total silence which lasted an eternity, until we heard, crackling over the airwaves, Armstrong's unforgettable words: "Houston, Tranquility Base here. The Eagle has landed."

We exploded into cheers, jumping up and down like kids and hugging each other. America was great! We had

won the space race to the moon! Despite Vietnam and
the urban riots, we could achieve great things if we
wanted, from curing polio to landing men on the moon.
I'll never forget the utter joy and happiness on the faces
of my family and friends as we watched Armstrong and
Aldrin hop about the moon surface taking photos of each
other. It was surreal, as if Dali himself had designed
lunar toys and tiny astronaut figures. I kept pinching
myself. Men on the moon -- on my birthday! My dad
said: "What a special birthday treat!" I couldn't believe
it; my eyes were moist with joy. In my trembling hands,
I held the science report that I had written ten years
earlier as a child. It was my passport to science and the
future, a guide to exploring the universe, and it had
guided me through math and science classes through the
1960s. It had allowed me to dream big dreams. It had
gotten me into Yale, one of the first Asian Americans to
get accepted. And now we had landed; the Eagle had
landed. We had achieved our dreams.

*Dream big and be prepared to do the long, hard work, but in the
end, it's worth it all.*

San Jose High School

Tucked away at the eastern edge of North San Jose, San Jose High is the oldest high school in San Jose and a blue-collar school heavily populated by a potpourri of minorities -- Mexican Americans, Afro Americans, Asian Americans, Native Americans, and recent immigrants from dozens of nations. We used to call it a mini-UN because of our diversity, which contrasted with the lily-white high schools in the West Valley. Despite sitting at the bottom of the academic rankings, we had pride, Bulldog Pride, a pride in our ethnic diversity and tolerance. Couples of mixed heritage were common during the 1960s when it was forbidden in most of the United States, let alone other California cities. The civil rights movement was underway and the racial barriers were falling slowly in the suburbs thanks to the Federal Highway Act, which sent families scurrying for better schools, parks and housing in the suburbs. San Jose in the "Valley of the Heart's Delight" led the way. From 1950, the city's population doubled every decade, turning the sleepy farm town into a miniature version of Los Angeles. In fact, City Manager Dutch Hamman bragged that San Jose would soon become another major city like LA and, years later, it achieved that dubious goal: a sprawling, faceless suburb covered with tract homes, freeways, and strip shopping malls.

My brothers, sisters and I wanted to leave San Jose and head for the suburbs with our friends, but my father was adamant about staying in town. He wanted us to study and grow up with a variety of people, not shield us in all-white suburbs. Instead of conceding, he hired a contractor to build a second story on our house for the master bedroom and my sister's bedroom. Our family, a pillar of the Japanese American community because he ran Nichi Bei Bussan (www.nbstore.com), a dry goods store converted during the 1960s into a Japanese gift shop, would not leave town. He would deepen our stakes in downtown by building and expanding, not fleeing for the suburbs. At the time, all of us children thought he was nuts. Why should we stay in the one of the worst high schools in San Jose when we could move to better ones in the suburb? But he never conceded and we resigned ourselves to staying in north San Jose. Years later, we would understand the wisdom of his decision. Many of our minority friends returned to San Jose, Berkeley and San Francisco after growing up in white suburbs, feeling totally alone, ignorant and alienated from their ethnic heritage. They only had white friends, while we had friends of all different colors and backgrounds. We were colorblind, not thinking about a person's color so much as their character, which Dr. Martin Luther King articulated in his famous "I Have a Dream" speech. Little did we know that my father, a YMCA International Committee member and a Methodist Church layman, shared that same dream, especially after our family and 120,000 other Japanese

Americans had been thrown into detention camps during World War II. His willingness to stand firm and support downtown San Jose from decline was his way of living his beliefs about the brotherhood of man.

Later, when I studied at Yale, it dawned on me what he intuitively knew. Most of my classmates were white and had led very sheltered lives, totally separate from ethnic minorities in the inner cities. They had no clue about what it meant to grow up a non-white person in America. They knew little, if anything, about the World War II camps. They had no understanding about why Blacks were rioting in the cities or why Native Americans were protesting on Alcatraz Island near San Francisco. Their sense of white privilege and superiority protected them from the harsh realities of American life. They only knew one side of America, the rich, powerful America with white picket fences, nice cars and college educations that we saw in the leafy engineering communities in the West Valley. I realized they lacked the social interaction and education that my father had wanted for us. He wanted us to live and truly understand the whole United States, not just suburbia, and become global citizens who could easily speak and empathize with people from around the world, as he did with his YMCA colleagues from Africa, Latin America, Asia, Europe and the Mideast. Like Dr. King, he was a man far ahead of his time.

Pioneers are usually laughed at for their visions and often attacked, so it requires courage to maintain one's bearings and leave footprints in the sands of time.

Launching Norman Mineta

Norman Mineta, the first successful Asian American politician from Silicon Valley, has led a Cinderella life, which has inspired other ethnic political leaders nationwide. I still remember the story that my father, Dave Tatsuno, told me about how he opened the door for Norm, as we all affectionately called him in San Jose's Japantown.

My father was not a very political person, even though he had graduated from UC Berkeley, served as president of the Japanese American Citizens League (JACL) chapter in San Francisco during the dark days after Pearl Harbor, and secretly shot home movies to document for posterity Topaz, Utah, one of the ten detention camps where Japanese Americans were interned during World War II -- the second home movie after the Zapruder film of the Kennedy assassination to be selected for inclusion in the Library of Congress' National Film Archives[1]. Despite the Great Depression, the camps, and losing a son from a tonsillectomy after the war, he was never bitter or angry, but was determined to improve his life and those of others. "T"is better to light a candle than to curse the dark," he would intone like a minister that he

---

1

http://www.nytimes.com/2006/02/13/national/13tatsu
no.html

always wanted to be. Although raised in the Methodist Church and YMCA, I could never fathom his stoic acceptance or Japanese *gaman* (perseverance) in the face of unfairness. Like other Americans, I was quick to protest and express my anger, but he was patient and forbearing, a Japanese Christian and a YMCA man, always thinking of other people. After the war, he had volunteered to help Japanese Americans returning from the camps who had lost all their property and belongings so they could rebuild their lives in the face of hostile neighbors. The camps and the return to California were traumatic for Japanese Americans and he was distraught over the mistreatment by the U.S. government. He was determined that it would never happen again.

As a board member of the San Jose Central YMCA, my father went for his daily swim and steam bath everyday at the Y. I would occasionally join him and we would sit around in the steam with local leaders -- city manager Ron James, police chief Ray Blackmore, city councilmen, department heads and corporate leaders – listening to talk about city policies, business, their families, and neighborhoods. For me it was an enlightening political education; I got a glimpse into the leaders guiding the growth of San Jose.

My Japanese American friends would often say I was very "white" because of my YMCA experiences, but my father wanted me to see how the valley operated. He would tell me that Japanese Americans needed to participate in society, not hide from it. We needed to leave the WWII camps behind and work with others to get ahead in life. But I was puzzled. On the one hand, he would let me spend Saturdays at all-white YMCA sports programs instead of attending Japanese language classes, but refused to move to an all-white suburb after the racial barriers came tumbling down. My brothers, sisters and I complained about his contradictions, which reflected the uncertainty his generation, the Nisei (second-generation Japanese Americans), felt about American society. They wanted to belong, yet did not feel welcome nor comfortable in the suburbs. They still acted and felt like second-class citizens. It was rare for a Japanese American or other non-whites to attain leadership positions in the valley, so we all remained safe within our ethnic enclaves.

My father was delighted when San Jose city manager Ron James asked him if he could recommend any eligible young Japanese Americans for an open position on the Human Rights Commission. My father immediately suggested Norman Mineta, a young Nisei born and raised in San Jose who had graduated from San Jose High School and UC Berkeley, but was working for his father's two-man insurance company in San Jose's Japantown. Norm was like an older brother. He helped around Wesley Methodist Church and always remembered your name and had something nice to say about your family. But beneath his cheerful façade, we all could see that he was frustrated staying within the tight-knit Japantown, a small "Meiji village" of modest shopkeepers, dentists, doctors and lawyers. Norm had bigger dreams. He wanted to go to law school and venture into the larger world like the rest of us young people, but lacked the money. Like many others after the war, he had to put his dreams aside to make a living.

For my father, Norm represented the future leadership of Japanese Americans. He was young, bright, likeable, and driven, the perfect person to lead our community and city. It was no surprise when Norm transformed the do-nothing Human Rights Commission into an activist organization that challenged racial discrimination in city policies and was later appointed by Ron James to an empty city council seat. Before we knew it, Norm was cutting ribbons and kissing babies as vice mayor. Everyone thought Norm was the mayor of San Jose because he acted like one. We were proud was the first mainland Nisei to enter the political mainstream.

But San Jose was caught in the past. When Norm ran for mayor, a San Jose Mercury editorial asked: "Are Japanese Americans ready for leadership?" Personally, I laughed at this condescension since Japanese in Japan, Hawaii and Sao Paolo were perfectly capable of running their own societies. Fortunately, San Jose voters liked Norm and voted him into office, making him the first Asian American mayor of a major American city, which was a real boost in Japantown. I was accepted by Yale, which sent shock waves through local high schools since no minority person in San Jose had ever been accepted by an Ivy League school. We had both achieved the American Dream. It was a joyous time, despite the Vietnam War and urban riots. We cheered as Norm opened council meetings, cut ribbons, and kissed more babies.

After eight years in office, Norm achieved another milestone; he was elected to Congress, the first Asian American from the mainland, where he represented Silicon Valley for two decades and co-founded the Congressional Asian Pacific American Caucus.

Soon after entering Congress, Norm asked my father for a favor. He wanted to serve on the House Public Works and Transportation Committee and wanted to borrow my father's notes from the San Jose Airport Commission meetings. More than happy to help Norm, my father lent him the notes, which Norm studied diligently. His hard work paid off. Ever the go-getter, Norman went far beyond our expectations. He served on the committee's aviation subcommittee between 1981 and 1988, chaired its Surface Transportation Subcommittee from 1989 to 1991, and served as chairman of the House Public Works and Transportation Committee between 1992 and 1994. After serving as vice president of Lockheed Martin Corporation, he was appointed in 2000 by President Clinton as the Commerce Secretary, the first Asian American to sit in the Cabinet. He had reached the pinnacle of American politics. My father beamed.

Along the way, Norm and his friend Republican Senate Whip Alan Simpson co-authored H.R. 442, the Civil Liberties Act of 1988, which officially apologized for and redressed the injustices endured by Japanese Americans during World War II. Few in the Japanese community thought it would pass. The audacity of requesting the United States to apologize for the World War II camps and request reparations was far beyond what even the boldest congressperson would dare.

When the bill passed, I remembered seeing my father cry for the first time in my life. He had always told me: "A samurai never cries." So his tears hit home. Norm had lifted the enormous weight of shame, frustration and anger from our shoulders. No longer were we second-class citizens. We were first-class Americans who could hold up our heads like others, thanks to Norm. My father's quiet persistence had finally paid off.

Norm's accomplishment had been an uphill battle. As he explained at a Japantown reception, most of Congress opposed the bill. The only reason they supported it was, as a southern Democrat told Norm, because of the heroism of the all-Japanese American 442nd Battalion, the most-decorated Army unit in U.S. military history, which had fought in Europe even though their families were incarcerated in camps. The 442nd lost 800 men in a valiant battle to save 200 men in the "Lost Texas Battalion," for which they were named Honorary Texans.

Norm was being modest. His friendly persuasiveness and sophisticated lobbying had won over the critical votes. In 1976, I visited Norm during spring break from graduate school and watched him in action. Norm invited me to watch from the upper gallery as Congress voted on bills. As he walked onto the floor of Congress, I remember congressmen greeting and clustering around him, a second-term congressman, as if he were a party leader. He was obviously an important person in Congress. My father reminded me that Norm's sister Helen was married to the brother of Mike Masaoka, the JACL representative in Washington D.C., who knew everyone important in town and had opened doors for Norm. Mike and my father had served as JACL presidents so they knew that Japanese Americans needed political leaders to protect us from vindictive, flag-waving politicians. But Mike could only open the door; he was in no position to win over the Congress. Having served as the San Jose JACL president, Norm had learned this lesson well. He got the votes and President Reagan went on to sign the bill, redressing one of the most flagrant violations of civil rights in U.S. history. My father was proud of Norm. He was the local boy who had done well. He had upheld the Constitution.

Open the doors to young, driven, dedicated people. Sometimes they will go farther than you can possibly imagine and leave an enduring legacy.

The 1980s PC Boom

Dataquest

Fast forward. 1982 - the eye of the tornado. Japanese memory chipmakers ran over Silicon Valley and dominated the news, stirring fear in business leaders and Washington D.C. Newspapers and magazines wrote about the "Japanese invasion" and showed cartoons of Godzilla threatening America.

At the time, I was working at Bechtel Corporation at its Washington D.C. office, ready to ship out to Cairo, Egypt to work as a loan administrator on the $1 billion El Shoubrah oil-fired power plant, but President Sadat was assassinated, ending my plans to work there. Due to rising radical fundamentalism, Americans were discouraged from working in Egypt and Bechtel wisely decided to replace us with Egyptians. My job went to an Egyptian American accountant. Saddened, my wife and I returned to San Jose, living with my parents due to the 12% unemployment rate. Jobs were scarce and I couldn't move back to San Francisco where we owned a house.

Although trained and working in urban planning, we wanted to return to San Francisco, but Bechtel was laying off people. The only place hiring was Silicon Valley and the only game in town was electronics. As an urban planner without a business degree, I thought it was a lost cause trying to find a job where one had to have a degree in engineering, software programming, marketing or accounting. But since 1975, I had followed Japan's VLSI (Very Large Scale Integration) project to develop a memory chip in order to compete with the Americans, just as I had followed the Apollo Project a decade earlier. In early 1981, leveraging their mass manufacturing prowess, the half dozen Japanese companies that had joined the VLSI Project – NEC, Hitachi, Toshiba, Fujitsu, Oki Electric and Mitsubishi Electric – began producing memory chips and ramped up production fast, reaching 30% share of the world market. Within eighteen months, they grabbed 70% market share, devastating Silicon Valley chipmakers who were forced to cut prices and lay off employees to survive. By December 1982, when I returned to Silicon Valley from Washington D.C. in the midst of the worst recession since the 1973-1975 oil crisis, the Japanese had thoroughly beaten us. The gloom was pervasive throughout the valley since it had pioneered the memory chip and now faced mounting layoffs.

Fortunately, before our return, my father asked if he should attend a UC Berkeley luncheon where Dr. Dan Klesken, manager of semiconductor information service at Dataquest, a high-tech market research firm, was speaking. I jumped at the opportunity and asked my father to get his business card. My father did, but forgot to return Dan's silver pen after writing down my name –

mistakenly or not, he didn't say. But it didn't matter; I called Dan to ask for an interview and returned his pen, which delighted him. He asked what I was doing. I told him I was looking for a job and thought Dataquest should launch a Japanese semiconductor service since Japan had thoroughly trounced the U.S. chipmakers. Dan smiled; he had just hired a former Motorola executive, Gene Norrett, to launch a Japanese service so I finagled to get an interview with both of them. Although I had no experience in the semiconductor industry, they were surprised that I knew all the industry buzzwords from tracking the VLSI Project. To get hired as a consultant, I cut them a deal: "You teach me everything about the semiconductor business and I'll teach you everything about Japan." Dan and Gene looked at each other a moment, then said: "OK, it's a deal."

Dataquest, founded in 1976 by former semiconductor executives, was the leading market research center for the electronics revolution. Started by four founders, it reached 400 employees by 1990 before the collapse in the syndicated market research business. Dataquest gathered every possible type of data – revenues, costs, shipments, component specifications, inventories, applications, user trends, etc. – in order to estimate company revenues and market shares since most companies never revealed their real data. Using multiple data sources and triangulation, we analysts could figure out actual sales within 3%, which astounded most executives.

For the next six months, my colleague Pat Cox and I met with Gene, who was bedridden in traction since he had slipped a disc lifting his daughter over his head, several times a week in his apartment to plan and prepare Dataquest's Japanese Semiconductor Industry Service (JSIS). It would be the first service in the world to track Japan's burgeoning chip industry. But we needed a Japanese expert. Our Dataquest Japan manager was an American who spoke limited Japanese and hung around the American Club. Gene fired him and searched for a Tokyo insider, identifying a Dempa Shimbun daily electronics reporter, Osamu Ohtake, who had covered the VLSI Project. Gene's interview was classic.

Gene: "Ohtake-san, how many business cards of semiconductor managers do you have?"

Ohtake: "Six thousand."

Gene: "How many do you use every year?"

Ohtake: "Three thousand."

Gene: "Can you show them to me?"

Ohtake-san went to a steel cabinet, opened a drawer, pulled out a binder marked "Fujitsu" on the edge, then opened it. The binder was filled with page after page of Fujitsu Semiconductor business cards in plastic pockets.

The drawer was filled with binders marked "NEC," "Hitachi," "Mitsubishi," "Sony," "Matsushita," etc.

Gene: "Ohtake-san, you're hired."

That was the single best hiring decision we ever made. Before we repositioned ourselves in Japan, industry experts warned us that Japan was a closed market and that Japanese chipmakers would never open their books to outsiders. Moreover, Keizai Shimbun, the daily financial and economic newspaper, had 10,000 employees and deep pockets so they could out-research and outsell us. But Gene had trained Hitachi's and NEC's top managers so he knew we could crack Japan with the right person -- Ohtake-san – who knew all of Japan's top semiconductor CEOs and managers. We hit the jackpot. Whenever we visited Tokyo, Ohtake-san called his colleagues to arrange appointments for us. Within a year, everyone knew us. Gene, whom the Japanese affectionately called "Noritsu-san" (Mr. Efficiency) because of his focused, no-nonsense approach, was soon on eating and drinking terms with them.

At our first Dataquest Japan conference in 1983, 75 Japanese and American semiconductor managers attended. Our conference attracted 150 in 1984, 300 in 1985 and 450 in 1986 at Japan's peak and our sales boomed. But at our 1985 conference in Kyoto, an official of the Ministry of International Trade and Industry (MITI) asked if Dataquest had hired security guards since all of Japan's top semiconductor executives were gathered in one room. When Gene said no, the official's face turned pale. If Japan's Red Army terrorist blew up a bomb in the room, it would have wiped out the entire Japanese semiconductor industry leadership. Gene later grinned; we had won! David had beaten Goliath. We had conquered the Japanese market with little money and only a handful of young insiders.

During the 1980s, Japan grew so quickly that trade conflicts bloomed across the industrial landscape from cars and semiconductors to steel and precision machinery. Our Japanese semiconductor group was inundated by calls from companies and the worldwide media for insights about the "Japan threat." I was constantly in the business news and called to testify to a Congressional panel about the future of American's high-tech competitiveness, where I was questioned about my loyalty because I was a messenger of bad news. Dataquest was so influential that experts called us a "private CIA" because we knew so much about the high-tech industry. Gene, Pat, Ohtake-san and I heard all the G2 (general gossip) in Tokyo, Silicon Valley, Seoul, Paris, London and Munich. We knew so much that Gene reminded us to play dumb so we wouldn't accidentally reveal industry secrets. Our names and quotes appeared weekly in the national and international media. The U.S.-Japan trade conflict reached a peak in 1987 and people constantly asked us if America would survive the Japanese onslaught. Did Silicon Valley have a future? Having grown up in San Jose, I rooted for the home team and felt Silicon Valley would always overcome the greatest challenges because of our openness, diversity, curiosity, drive and speed. We attracted the top brains from around the world in electronics so we would always innovate our way out of a rut.

But at the time, it wasn't so obvious. Japan had bludgeoned our industries and appeared to be taking over the world, with its buyout of Rockefeller Center and Columbia Pictures. Pundits stated, "Japan uber alles"; Japan had won. Whenever I visited Tokyo, Japanese managers would privately scorn "the American disease," predicting the U.S. had peaked and would decline before Japan's dominance. As a Japanese American, whose parents had been thrown into World War II camps because of Pearl Harbor, it was a bitter pill to swallow. I was the messenger of bad news and secretly wanted Japan to fail. Little did I know that a few years later, Japan's economy would collapse and struggle for 15 years in a prolonged, self-imposed recession. The Japanese Century would only last ten years.

Hire insiders if you want to conquer foreign markets and never let hubris blind your decision-making.

Acer's Stan Shih

The City of Milpitas on the eastern shore of San Francisco Bay used to be an agricultural town filled with blue-collar folks working at the GM plant in Fremont, fruit packing companies, shipping companies and warehouses dotting the East Bay and San Jose -- down-to-earth people who enjoyed the California life of small ranch houses, backyard barbeques and ball games at the local parks and schools.

One day, my Dataquest boss, Gene Norrett, invited me to lunch with a newcomer in town, Stan Shih, the CEO of a small Taiwanese electronics assembly company. I went along, always happy to meet his colleagues and slurp some good noodles. We went to a tiny noodle shop, one of the few in Milpitas, which was then dominated by sandwich shops. Unlike today, Asians were rare in Milpitas back in the early 1980s so the little noodle shop stood out like a sore thumb.

Stan and Gene got into an intense discussion about the business opportunities for PC and electronics assembly, but I remember Stan saying: "The trouble with most Taiwanese companies is that they're mom-and-pop operations. They only hire friends and family and totally want to control their little companies, so they never grow very big. They all end up competing with each other doing the same thing. I don't want Acer to be like that. I want to build it into an international company like IBM. What do you think?"

Gene was very frank and got to the point: "Stan, you want to become an IBM? Then think like IBM. Hire the best people and run it like an international company. Come to Silicon Valley and we'll help you."

I still remember Gene's wise words: "If you want to become an IBM, then think like IBM." Be of the world, by the world, for the world! Gene agreed that the problem of many Silicon Valley and Taiwanese entrepreneurs is that they ran their little companies like fiefdoms, hiring only friends and family, never sharing much equity or authority, and content to be "big fish in a little pond." So they rarely grew into major corporations.

But Stan was different; he had fire in his eyes. He clearly didn't want Acer to remain another no-name mom-and-pop company; he wanted to become a new IBM. So he signed up as a Dataquest client and often dropped by our offices and conferences to learn all he could about global markets.

I was not involved with Stan Shih after those initial meetings, but I still remember his intense eyes and passionate voice. He wanted Acer to be great, not just another little Taiwanese copycat company. He wanted to show the world that Taiwanese could be industry leaders. He reminded me of Applied Materials' CEO Jim Morgan and our Japanese, South Korean and Singapore clients, who intensely grilled us Dataquest research analysts and managers and networked with semiconductor industry leaders for all the market insights they could gather.

So it was no surprise that within several years, Acer had become the leading Taiwanese electronics manufacturer and, despite setbacks during the 1990s, regained a leading position in the PC business in 2008. For Stan Shih, it was not just about building better, cheaper PCs, but about national and personal pride, about being able to stand with his head up in this competitive global economy. Over time, Stan led Taiwan's electronics industry to become the leading manufacturer of electronics products, from PCs and cell phones to MP3 players and LCD panels. But even today, very few companies have the global name brand and reputation of Acer, which still stands as one of the few Taiwanese companies to break out of the pack. Most of Stan's competitors no longer exist today.

Aim high and avoid falling into the trap of hiring just friends and family. Hire slowly and only hire the best, then paint the vision and let your team execute.

Applied Materials

Silicon Valley entrepreneurs, like industry pioneers
anywhere, are passionate, forceful people who refuse to
bow to conventional thinking. They are like forces of
nature, unbound and untamable. Jim Morgan, founder
and CEO of Applied Materials, was like that: solid,
handsome, strong and visionary. I remember the day he
walked into Dataquest and met with my boss Gene and
me. He reminded me of tall-walking, straight-talking
farmers from my childhood who worked hard and had
dirt under their nails.

Jim said he wanted to enter the Japanese market, but
other industry leaders said it was Mission Impossible.
The Japanese market was closed to foreigners, especially
to semiconductor equipment makers like Applied
Materials, because of the close *keiretsu* ties between
chipmakers, equipment makers, and financiers. After
World War II, Japan had mastered mercantilist trade
policies, exporting to its way to recovery and growth
while blocking foreign imports. Japan's postwar
industrial history was replete with cases where foreign
companies were stymied and frustrated by its
bureaucrats who laid every possible trap and barrier in
the way to block foreign products and services. Aiming
to jumpstart and rebuild the Japanese economy, the U.S.
government supported these trade barriers, but they
were beginning to hurt our leading industries, as the

DRAM business collapse had shown. U.S. manufacturers had to penetrate the Japanese market or they would be at a competitive disadvantage against Japanese companies that were entering the U.S. market.

Jim shared those feelings; Applied Materials was a small company that had to succeed in Japan, where the future of the semiconductor industry was located. Booming PC sales were driving memory chip sales and semiconductor equipment up the industrial food chain, so he was determined to crack the Japanese market. Jim knew it was Mission Impossible, but he loved tough challenges. He signed up for our Dataquest Japanese semiconductor service and, like a diligent student, studied the Japanese market rigorously, reading all our market reports and newsletters, asking questions, attending conferences and grilling our analysts. I'll never forget the intense concentration on his face, which contrasted with his country boy demeanor. He was like Henry Fonda walking into Dataquest – relaxed, confident, curious, friendly and intense. He was the perfect customer who knew exactly what he wanted and a paragon for how Silicon Valley became such a great industrial power. He had focus and concentration.

Needless to say, Applied Materials was the first foreign semiconductor equipment maker to successfully enter the Japanese market, which Jim and his son Jeff later wrote about in their book "Cracking the Japanese Market." Applied Materials would earn half of its revenues in

Japan and was deeply respected by Japanese chipmakers for its high quality and service. At Dataquest conferences, I remember Jim schmoozing with Hitachi, NEC and other company executives, who had become his friends. Jim had shown the world that it was indeed possible to crack the Japanese market; it just took a lot of hard work, study, diligence and perseverance – traits that had built America, Japan, Taiwan and South Korea.

I remember Gene saying: "These semiconductor guys mostly come from modest backgrounds so they have their feet firmly planted on the ground. A lot of them are farm boys who like working with their hands and former military officers who understand self-discipline. That's how Silicon Valley was built."

Keep your eyes open for young people with passion, conviction, curiosity, and a no-nonsense willingness to work hard. They often do the impossible and create new companies and industries.

Bangalore

India was never much in the news during the early
1980s. Everything in high tech was happening in the
U.S., Europe, Japan, and the Four Tigers. Even though
I worked on Dataquest's Asian electronics service, India
never registered on my radar until Prakash Chandra, the
president of the Silicon Valley Indian Professional's
Association (SIPA.org), approached me and invited me
to meet the Indian consul general in San Francisco who
wanted to ask me some questions. Having advised the
Taiwanese, Singapore and Hong Kong governments
about their high-tech initiatives, I figured they wanted to
develop India's high-tech industry strategy.

As I expected, the consul general asked about Japan and
the Four Tigers and how I saw their futures. But then he
mentioned Texas Instruments' small chip design center
that had recently opened in Bangalore, a small village in
southwestern India, wondering if TI's business model
was expandable. At the time, many semi-custom
chipmakers were setting up design centers in Europe to
accelerate development by taking advantage of the time
difference so the company could work around the clock.
European programmers could work while Americans
slept and vice versa. Chipmakers were looking at
Taiwan, where computer makers sourced their computer
motherboards, but nobody had opened a center in India.

The consul general said Bangalore wanted to become another Silicon Valley, except focused on software, and wondered if it was possible.

"Of course," I replied. " Except you need to lay fiber optic cables since satellite time is very expensive and you'll eventually need more capacity."

"But Bangalore is only a tiny village," he asked. "Will anybody come?"

"When I was a child, Silicon Valley was just farmland. People laughed at us and called us country bumpkins. So anything is possible. You just have to plan for it."

The consul general was delighted and proposed meeting several times more with SIPA managers to discuss how Bangalore could be developed. I gave him whatever insights I could about the booming PC and semiconductor industries, the role of Japan and the Four Tigers, and how Bangalore could become the next Silicon Valley. Like diligent students, he, Prakash and their colleagues diligently took notes.

So for the next year or two, SIPA managers and I brainstormed the future of Bangalore. We met the Bangapore research park manager, who showed photos of the tiny research labs in the middle of farmland, reminding me of the Stanford Research Park in 1960, asking how he could build Bangalore into another Silicon Valley. To be frank, I was unsure whether he would succeed. India was so poor, totally unlike Northern California with Stanford, Berkeley, UC San Francisco and other top universities and colleges and billions of dollars of Pentagon and venture capital money flowing into it. Besides a few foreign chipmakers, I could not see how Bangalore would ever generate enough business to build a Silicon Valley, which shows how limited my imagination was. All I remember is encouraging the Indian consul general, SIPA and the Bangalore research park manager that India had a future in software, what future I did not know, but I remember telling them: "It took us over 40 years to create Silicon Valley. If you work hard, perhaps you can build Bangalore into a leading center in 20 years."

Little did I realize at the time that we were discussing the future of India's software industry and that Bangalore would become the Silicon Valley of India. At best, I thought the village would attract perhaps a hundred semi-custom chip design centers, not the software industry behemoth that it would eventually become.

Sometimes, big things come in small packages -- like personal computers, Stanford Research Park, Japan's Akihabara electronic bazaar, and the Internet. They come into the world like newborn babies, bare and unimpressive, more suitable for hobbyists and techies than serious business people.

Never underestimate the power of passion and vision; sometimes redwood seeds grow into trees taller than you can possibly imagine.

Saving Intel

In 1984, PC and memory chip markets collapsed worldwide, taking down hundreds of ventures and companies in Silicon Valley. Even Intel, the mighty pioneer, was feeling the heat, with its memory business losing badly to the Japanese memory chipmakers. I knew Intel's situation was bad, but not as dire as I thought. One day, my boss Gene Norrett at Dataquest, the leading market research company in the semiconductor industry, invited me to join him for lunch with our client, Ron Whittier, Senior VP at Intel, who wanted to talk about the market situation.

We went to a nice restaurant in Milpitas and were settling down to our salad when Ron dropped the bomb on us: "We're going under. Intel is going under in six months. We're bleeding badly. We're going bankrupt." I choked on my salad and dropped my fork. "The troika (Intel founders Gordon Moore, Robert Noyce, and Andy Grove) doesn't know what to do. We don't have many options left."

Gene and I stared at each other with disbelief. Intel going bankrupt -- impossible! It was a national treasure, one of the pioneers of the chip revolution and Silicon Valley. Its failure would cause havoc on Wall Street and Washington D.C. and total fear in Silicon Valley. Our local hero was going down! I worried about the political and social response to Intel failing, fearing another round of "Japan bashing" among populists and protectionists and its attendant fallout on Asian Americans, but this time led by Silicon Valley's powerful elite. Detroit was a rustbelt dinosaur, but Silicon Valley represented America's future. Without it, we were in serious, serious trouble.

For the next three lunch meetings, Ron explained the details about the situation, saying that only six people in the world knew about Intel's plight – the Troika and the three of us – and asked us not to breathe a word to anyone at Dataquest or at home, lest Intel's stock price collapse. Gene turned to me, warning: "Loose lips sink ships." So I listened carefully and kept mum. At Dataquest, we heard all the industry G2 (general gossip) about mergers, acquisitions, bankruptcies, financings, internal battles, job transfers, business strategies and other insider news, but this situation was cataclysmic. It potentially signaled that Japan had beaten America in high tech, something that would knock the wind out of our competitive sails. If Intel failed, America would lose its prime Silicon Valley leader; our generals would be gone.

Our lunch meetings with Ron ended somberly, almost like a death wake, and we kept totally silent. It was hard for me to not to look depressed around Dataquest analysts, friends and family because Intel was one of my accounts and I was so emotionally attached to the company, which represented everything great about

Silicon Valley – the flat organization, the camaderie, the no-nonsense thinking and discussions, the can-do, will-do attitude. I couldn't imagine a Silicon Valley without Intel, just as one cannot imagine Hollywood without Disney or New York City without Times Square. It was a global icon, a symbol of all that was wonderful about American entrepreneurialism and technology. Now it was going under. I felt a sick, sinking sensation, like the navigator who had failed the captain of the Titanic. If Intel went under, I could never forgive myself because it would have happened on my watch. I was the Japanese semiconductor expert hired to provide knowledge so companies could compete and survive against the Japanese juggernaut. I would have failed the most famous of all Silicon Valley companies. The pressure was enormous and I couldn't sleep at night.

One morning, Gene called me into his office. He was on a conference call with Ron, who wanted to know what we, Dataquest, recommended to the Troika. Dataquest knew more about Intel's competitors – the Japanese semiconductor industry – than anyone else in the world. Gene said we would discuss and think it over. Hanging up, Gene turned to me and asked what Intel should do. I said: "Shut down their memory production lines. They already lost the memory market to Japan. They should put all their wood behind microprocessors, with a little bit into telecom chips. It's their only chance." The PC market was growing fast so I reasoned that Intel should position itself as the leading microprocessor supplier.

Gene agreed, saying, "I was thinking the same thing." He called back Ron, telling him our advice, but Ron replied, "We can't shut down half the company and lay off thousands of people. Wall Street will go nuts." Gene said: "We think it's a no-brainer. Either you shut down half the company now or the whole company in six months." There was silence on the phone. Ron said he would tell the Troika and get back to us.

The wait was unbearable and I couldn't sleep well. It was like a deathwatch. A few days later, Ron called back and told us: "The Troika agrees. We're shutting down the memory business. Don't say a word." Gene and I looked at each other with a mixture of happiness and fear. The Troika, the most famous entrepreneurs in Silicon Valley, was actually listening to our advice. We held our breath, praying that Intel would succeed. If not, we would have failed the biggest challenge of our times.

After an interminable wait, Intel announced two weeks later that it was shutting down its memory lines. Headlines screamed the news. The media went wild and we were bombarded day after day for our comments and insights. Gene and I pretended to be surprised and repeated what we thought: Intel had already lost its memory business to the Japanese and should focus on microprocessors.

Intel did not still, but moved fast -- very, very fast. For the next year, Intel's top strategists and engineers came swarming into Dataquest several times a week in order to craft its microprocessor strategy with Ken McKenzie, a former Zilog engineer who was our key microprocessor analyst. I remember Ken taking on the task of saving Intel with a mixture of joy, determination and uneasiness. The future of Intel and Silicon Valley depended on his insights and advice. Never had some much pressure weighed on a single Dataquest analyst. Of course, our entire semiconductor group pitched in, but Ken was the point man in Intel's comeback.

The rest is history. In a few years, Intel built a lucrative microprocessor business and became, as Gene, Ken and I had envisioned, the world's leader in microprocessors. Silicon Valley regained its swagger and our team was proud once again to be Americans. When Ron Whittier visited Dataquest, Gene congratulated him and the Troika, saying: "You guys did a great job." Ron grinned, saying we all did it together. We all saved Intel.

Andy Grove is right; only the paranoid survive in high tech. Never let your guard down and get complacent, and never give up. Focus on your strengths and go for it if you want to become world class. Only the brave thrive.

Samsung's DRAM strategy

If the Japanese chipmakers sank the American memory chip business, the Koreans were the next in line to challenge the U.S. and Japan. As the U.S.-Japan semiconductor trade war heated up, with the Semiconductor Industry Association (SIA) claiming that Japan was dumping memory chips by pricing them below production costs, Samsung – a major conglomerate heavily subsidized by the South Korean government like rivals Hyundai, Goldstar, and Daewoo – was planning its DRAM (dynamic random access memory) memory chip strategy. Except this time, I would be directly involved. Samsung announced it would invest $5 billion in the memory business, an enormous sum, which could build nearly five Intel factories. Samsung hired Dataquest as a consultant to help them craft their DRAM strategy. Their goal: beat Japan.

For the next year, Lane Mason, the memory chip expert at Dataquest, and I would meet with Samsung strategy planning researchers and managers who came in almost everyday to gather information about the memory chip business, Japanese competitors, and marketing strategies. At the time, Samsung's mission appeared quixotic. The Koreans could produce steel and ships, but not high-tech products like chips and computers. There were many doubts in many quarters, but others feared Samsung because of its size and government backing. Korea Inc. was now challenging Japan Inc.

Other Dataquest analysts disliked helping an American rival and worried about losing critical business intelligence to Samsung researchers, who were always walking about the floor. Several times, it got tense when some analysts accused Samsung of stealing market research data from the desks of our analysts and we were forced to warn them not to go unescorted through the office. There never was evidence that Samsung took anything, but this incident reflected the underlying tension at the time. The U.S. chip industry was struggling with Japanese memory chip price "dumping" and the Toshiba incident where critical propeller grinding technology was given to the Soviet Union, raising major fears in Washington D.C. about Japan's "leaky bucket." South Korea was a loyal ally, there were fears in Silicon Valley and Washington D.C. of Koreans entering and controlling the semiconductor business, which is critical to the U.S. military. And ironically, Dataquest was sitting in the middle of this global high-tech tension, with customers from all the nations involved. They were clients who walked into our offices week after week, sitting down with our analysts to learn all they could about how to win in the semiconductor business.

Semiconductor clients sometimes joked that Dataquest was a private version of the CIA since we were insiders who knew so much about the high-tech industry. With 30 high-tech fields covered by our analysts, we heard all the G2 (general gossip) about the industry and its players in advance. My boss Gene rarely read the newspaper, saying that he heard it six months earlier through the grapevine. He said: "You and I would make lousy CIA operators because we're so visible in the media and talk too much. Spies look like IBM salesmen; they're clean-cut, wear suits, and blend in with the woodwork. Moreover, the CIA pays spies for information and doesn't make it public. By contrast, clients share information with Dataquest and pay us to summarize, analyze and make it public. We accept money of all different colors, as long as it's legal and ethical."

Gene would burst into laughter, which would echo through the office, his face turning beet red, and I would end up with a sore stomach from laughing so hard. Never did I have a fun boss like Gene, who had so much insight about people in the industry. Our team had years of fun working together, advising our clients from around the world how to understand, compete and partner with the Japanese chipmakers and how to enter the Japanese market. It was the most fun job that I've ever had. Even now, we Dataquest analysts wax lyrical about the good ole days at Dataquest when we worked together like one big, happy family, helping each other out and enjoying lunches and picnics together. It was the good times in Silicon Valley when it still was a family where people cared about technology and each other more than just money.

So we helped Samsung put together its $5 billion DRAM market entry strategy and watched as the company built new factories and shipped memories through 1986 when the U.S. Department of Commerce imposed dumping tariffs on Japanese memory chip makers, ultimately outshipping the Japanese.

I heard from Lane that Samsung had reverse-engineered the 1Megabit DRAM chip, but not on a computer. Instead, Samsung engineers had projected a copy of a Japanese chip on a huge piece of paper on the wall, then drew over the chip lines and photographed it! We all laughed at their archaic method, but it worked, beautifully as we would later discover.

Just before the U.S. government imposed tariffs on Japanese memory chips, Gene recommended buying and stockpiling DRAMs, which he predicted would jump in price from $1.60 at least three or four times. He underestimated; the prices skyrocketed over $10 so investors who anticipated the market made a fortune overnight.

Samsung eventually surpassed the Japanese chipmakers in DRAM shipments and remains to this day a memory chip leader. Gene and I still remember the good times when we would meet Samsung and tell them that the Japanese were tough, but beatable.

Technology markets come in waves, often affected by political events, so always keep your eyes open for what happens in the major capitals around the world.

Dell Computer

One of the most amazing entrepreneurs I've ever spoken to was Michael Dell. I still remember the morning he called me while I was working for Dataquest as a telecommuter. A young man introduced himself, saying George Kozmetsky, the co-founder of aerospace systems company Teledyne Corporation, the founder of the IC2 Institute in Austin, Texas and the richest man in Austin, had referred him. I knew George from 1987 when he invited me to speak at his Technopolis conference in Austin about regional technology parks. George's goal was to create the "Austin Miracle" – to turn Austin into a high-tech industrial center – so he championed entrepreneurial research and workshops to promote his vision, which ultimately bore fruit. Perhaps not too surprisingly, Michael asked George to be his mentor.

I asked Michael what he was doing and he mentioned that he had started a PC assembly business in his dorm room at the University of Texas at Austin, where he was a pre-med major but planned to drop out since his assembly business was getting too busy. His dorm room looked like a workshop, with PC parts cramming the place. Trucks and friends delivered finished PCs to student and faculty customers on campus, making it inconvenient and unacceptable to campus officials, so he planned to move his new company, Dell Computer, to a storefront and started manufacturing in volume. He called me to ask for introductions to people in Silicon Valley and Japan.

What struck me about Michael was his intensity and self-confidence. He said that since childhood he could sell anything, but I told him that PC assembly was a lousy business since hundreds of venture capital-funded PC companies were failing. Michael disagreed, saying it was a great business, generating 40% gross margins. With total disbelief, I asked him how that was possible.

"Build-to-order," Michael replied. "I'm reversing the whole process. Instead of building the PCs first, building up huge inventories, and selling them before their prices drop, I sell first, bank the money, make the PCs, then ship. It's like a self-service sandwich shop. I'm turning PCs into a service business."

Michael explained there were 50,000 students and faculty on campus, all who would need a PC. His buddies, who disliked working for minimum wages, were his sales team. They would get a 10% sales commission for closing orders and bringing $2,000 upfront in cash and the other 10% for delivering it across campus since he disliked carrying heavy PCs. He was generating lots of cash. In fact, at the time we spoke, he had $10,000 in cash on his desk from orders that morning. He ran to the bank everyday with thousands of dollars, so the bank thought he was running an illegal business. He claimed he was generating $80,000 a month in sales, which was doubling every month.

I was impressed, but still unconvinced about his business model. He could produce dozens of PCs a month, but competitors could easily copy him and put him out of business. Michael said he and a UT Austin engineering professor of manufacturing had designed a build-to-order PC factory based on Toyota's "kanban" method of just-in-time (JIT) delivery. I was stunned, having never heard of a pre-med student design a "factory of the future." Steve Jobs was legendary, but Apple used a traditional manufacturing approach. Michael was turning the PC business upside down. A shiver went down my neck, as I realized that I was talking to a business genius. Michael had more "street smarts" than hundreds of entrepreneurs whom I had met in Silicon Valley. He reminded me of another PC recycler I met at an Aspen Institute conference who rebuilt used IBM and became one of Fortune magazine's top entrepreneurs.

Nevertheless, I still wasn't convinced that Michael could succeed where hundreds of other ventures had failed against major PC manufacturers. I asked him: "IBM, HP, NEC or Compaq could build a build-to-order factory and blow you away in a week. How could ever survive?"

I still remember Michael's reply: "You're a Dataquest market analyst, right? Now suppose you were the VP of marketing/sales at any PC maker in the world and went before the board to say: 'Gentlemen, as of today, we're shutting down all our production lines, firing our sales teams, and eliminating our distributors. Instead, we will build a new build-to-order factory and sell direct using 800 phone numbers because a kid named Michael Dell in Austin is doing it. How long would you last in the company?'"

He was right. I replied: "About two minutes and the board would hand you your head on a plate." No marketing VP in her right mind would ever destroy her company's business model in order to copy a young kid untested in global competition.

Michael laid out his vision. "I don't think there's any CEO, board or VP of marketing in the world with the guts to copy me. In fact, I think it will take at least 5 to 10 years for PC manufacturers to wake up to my business model and by then I'll be long gone." I counted; it took over 5 years for IBM, HP, Compaq and others to copy Dell's build-to-order business model, but by then Dell was a major player.

I asked Michael what his business goal was. He replied: "To eliminate every PC middleman in America." But as our phone call came to an end, he secretly confided: "My real goal is to become the biggest PC maker in America by the year 2000." I remember snickering to myself. A kid in a storefront beating the world's top PC makers. It would never happen. Even Apple had few big competitors in the beginning.

The rest is history. A few months before 2000, Dell became the #1 PC manufacturer in the United States. The kid would beat Silicon Valley and Taiwan by totally turning the PC business upside down. Who would ever guessed that a premed dropout from UT Austin would have beaten Fortune 100 corporations at their own game? It was unthinkable, like a B-grade Hollywood movie. But Michael Dell would not be the last young entrepreneur whom I would meet. He was just the beginning of a line of young entrepreneurs who would go on to create fortunes and become business legends.

Never underestimate smart, driven, focused young people. They may overturn and transform entire industries and nations.

Japan's Technopolis and "Japanophobia"

In 1982, the Japan External Trade Organization (JETRO) published a white paper describing its new Technopolis program, a national plan to "clone" Silicon Valley by developing 26 science parks. After Japanese memory chipmakers had demolished the Americans, this program took on ominous significance for American industry leaders and policymakers who feared a Japanese takeover of the critical high-tech industry. The semiconductor and computer boom had ignited worldwide competition for the next generation of high-tech researchers and industries, stimulating other nations to try to clone Silicon Valley with their own technology parks, an effort that continues today.

In 1976, I had applied to Harvard's Graduate School of Design (GSD) to enroll in its PhD program in urban planning. Having taught English and studied Japanese language and urban planning in Okayama for two years, my goal was to study Japanese urban and environmental problems, but I was too early. The GSD admissions officer suggested that I enroll in the Japanese program, but it was focused on literature, history, politics and sociology, not urban planning or public policy. Even Harvard Business School lacked courses on Japanese management practices until the early 1980s. I enrolled in the urban planning program and gave up my idea of researching Japanese urban policies, so my interest was piqued when I read about MITI's Technopolis program.

To my good fortune, I got a book contract from Reston Publishing in Virginia through an introduction by a San Jose State University business student, whom I had engaged to prepare a business plan for my consulting firm. The computer book editor was expanding into business books and was intrigued by Japan, so he gave me a contract. He and his wife wanted to see Japan and asked to join me on one of my research trips to the Technopolis sites, which turned out to be a pleasant way to see Japan and gauge the reaction of local officials who were running active marketing campaigns to bring in foreign companies and investors. Although I did all my research and interviewing in Japanese, overcoming the big cultural divide was a big challenge for me since I'm not formally trained in interpreting and translating, but learned on the job and from my wife.

During my business trips to Dataquest Japan, I visited the Ministry of International Trade and Industry (MITI), which oversaw JETRO's offshore activities and ran the innocuous-sounding Japan Industrial Location Center (JILC) to develop the Technopolis program. Located in the Toranomon district of Tokyo near the Japanese ministries in Kasumigaseki, JILC was a treasure trove of data on Japan's industrial parks and Technopolis programs. During the next few years, the JILC took me under its wing and gave me most of their planning reports for the Technopolis program and arranged for me to visit eighteen of the Technopolis parks so I could see firsthand how they had implemented their plans.

To my delight, I was able to enjoy eating and drinking through the eighteen Technopolis regions during my weeklong tours after doing Dataquest business in Tokyo and Osaka. The prefectural planning offices were welcoming and efficient, arranging for me to interview their top Technopolis planning teams, meet political officials and tour their techparks. Between 1984 and 1986, I probably visited over 50 Japanese cities and towns throughout the country, learning how Japan was implementing its high-tech manufacturing and research plans, and wrote a book, "The Technopolis Strategy", which was published by HarperCollins in 1986. I saw how organized, systematic and holistic the Japanese were in their thinking and planning, being much more influenced by MITI and other national government agencies than planning agencies in the United States and, as a result, much more conformist.

Like Japanese students wearing school uniforms, the Technopolis plans all looked alike to me. Despite some local differences, each region emphasized the same virtues about relatively cheap labor, educated labor, fresh water, and open space. Later, I learned many had used the same Tokyo consulting firms, which basically did cookie-cutter plans. Despite the lack of originality, their plans were bold, with each region planning to invest

$3 billion to $5 billion on infrastructure spending for roads, airports, highways, telecommunications, research facilities, housing, university extension programs, parks and community centers. They were planned like urban gardens, reminding me of the "City Beautiful" urban planning movement in the United States in the 1920s and 1930s. Besides Silicon Valley, Technopolis planners had visited the beautiful science parks of Cambridge, England, the Research Triangle in North Carolina, and the Sophia Antipolis outside of Nice, France. Later, the French responded by creating thirty "Technopoles" of its own and I was often invited by these Technopoles to comment on their plans.

I discovered the power of the Technopolis concept in 1987 when the Chinese ambassador to the United Nation visited Silicon Valley to speak at an invitation-only luncheon with a few dozen-tech managers. I gave him my Technopolis book, which was fresh off the press, but he said he had already read it – in Chinese. In fact, he said my book was popular in Beijing among government officials who were in the midst of planning their free economic zones and science parks.

Later, my publisher called and proudly announced that she was holding a check for $1,800 from the Chinese publisher of my book, but she would frame it instead of cashing it. When I asked why, she replied: "They must have really liked your book and made a lot of money. It's the first check that any New York publisher has ever received from China." Piracy has always been a problem there so the check was a signature event. Perhaps Chinese publishers might pay someday for books in translation.

So Japan, which has been a model for China and other developing nations because it has been able to retain its culture despite modernization, provided China with a model for its high-tech parks: Western science and Eastern spirit.

The Technopolis concept was not just influential in Japan, France, China and other science parks around the world. It was a major topic of concern in Washington D.C.

By 1985, "Japanophobia" was running rampant in the United States. Japanese chipmakers were dominating markets and buying up Hawaii. Intel was going bankrupt. Business Week and Time splashed headlines about the Japanese "invasion", harkening back to World War II. As a Japanese American whose family had been thrown into the detention camp in Topaz, Utah south of Salt Lake City during the war, this xenophobia worried me. In 1982, Vincent Chin, a young Chinese American, had been mistaken for Japanese and murdered by angry autoworkers in Detroit, which sent fear through the Asian American communities. Would we also be targeted by angry, racist skinheads or unemployed workers? Would vandals ride by at night and shoot at our living room windows? Racism in America was alive and well and, as a Japanese American reporting on the status of the Japanese electronics industry for Dataquest, I was the messenger of bad news who was often viewed as anti-American.

The high point came when I was asked to testify about Technopolis and the "Japanese threat" to a Congressional panel. I had just been interviewed by the McNeil-Lehrer reporter and was questioned by the congressmen. One asked: "Mr. Tatsuno, who's side are you for? Ours or theirs?" I could scarcely believe my ears. During World War II, Japanese Americans had been questioned about our loyalty in the infamous Questions 27 and 28 in the detention camps when the Army asked whether we would forswear allegiance to the Japanese Emperor and fight for the U.S. armed forces. Most camp internees declared their loyalty, but some – known as the "No-No Boys" – refused to answer and were thrown into isolation camps for disloyalty. The schism created by those questions still split the Japanese American community to this day between the "200% Americans" and the "disloyal."

Sitting there, I remember telling the congressman who questioned my loyalty: "If I were French American, you probably wouldn't ask that question." It was a very tense moment and I still remember the angry and indignation at being asked the question. The congressman was miffed, but his question reminded me of the thinking that threw my parents and 120,000 Japanese Americans into concentration camps during World War II.

A few years earlier, I had sat in an after-dinner reception of businessmen with Congressman John Dingle of Michigan, who was asked about Japan. As a representative of the layoff-stricken Detroit, he talked about how the United States needed to protect its labor force. But then added "those yellow-belly people" in his answer. I could scarcely believe my ears that he would use such racist words in a public setting, but then it didn't surprise me. Anti-Japanese sentiment was at fever pitch in Detroit.

The worry over the competitiveness of the U.S. semiconductor industry was at an all-time high. The Office for Technology Assessment (OTA), a now-defunct research arm for the White House, was one of our Dataquest clients. In 1987, I was invited to speak to OTA officials and invited guests. I'll never forget the meeting. I walked into the room and was greeted by several dozen officials from different government agencies. As I walked around the room shaking hands, I handed each official my business card, but most of them apologized, saying they didn't have a business card. I asked them why. The OTA manager replied: "It's alphabet soup here today." Alphabet soup? What did he mean by that? All the officials laughed. "We have the FBI, CIA, DIA, NSA, Army Intelligence, Navy

Intelligence, Secret Service, and security agencies that the American public has never heard of." I was stunned since I recognized many of the faces from conferences and trade shows in Silicon Valley.

My Dataquest boss Gene Norrett was right, but I never had proof of it. Silicon Valley was filled with intelligence agencies, both American and foreign, and the valley was one big "cat and mouse" game between these agencies over America's high-tech secrets. The Soviet consulate in San Francisco bristling with antennas and receivers aimed at Silicon Valley was well known, but other countries were more discrete. They usually sent spies as commercial officers and cultural attaches. With Lawrence Livermore Labs designing nuclear weapons and the Pentagon spending billions of dollars a year in Silicon Valley technologies, the stakes are high. Indeed, the Pentagon and Department of Energy has always funded much of the advanced technologies in Silicon Valley through top-secret projects, which has served as a form of state-run "venture capital", but Silicon Valley leaders have rarely acknowledged this heavy, on-going funding, except for Steve Blank who has written a nice history of the Pentagon's involvement in Silicon Valley. Many still like to believe that Silicon Valley was purely the creation of entrepreneurs creating products in their garage. That was half true, but the Pentagon, DOE and now Homeland Security play major roles in leading-edge research and development.

So as I left the OTA office and walked past the White House, I felt a sense of surprise and pride at my tiny role in the struggle to save America's high-tech industry. I was just a foot soldier in the bigger global battle, a market research analyst who just happened to know a lot because of my pivotal role at Dataquest. I felt like the Japanese American men who had served General MacArthur during World War II in the Military Intelligence School (MIS) out of San Francisco's Presidio and Fort Savage, Minnesota. My intelligence was critical in saving America's semiconductor industry, at least at the time. During the 1990s, Japan's economy went into a deep recession, ending the "Japan threat" in Silicon Valley. The once-feared Godzilla was now a struggling giant trying to save itself from decline in the face of a bigger giant – China.

Books are powerful so be careful what you write. Words have the power to influence people and affect millions of lives.

Cloning Silicon Valley

Silicon Valley's skyrocketing growth triggered a boom in government initiatives around the world to clone Silicon Valley.   More than 1,000 science and business parks were being built, many by members of the International Association of Science Parks (www.iasp.org). My Technopolis book became an unofficial guidebook for IASP members who wanted to understand Silicon Valley's success and how government might intervene like Japan. They wanted to know the secret sauce. They thought it was a simple recipe of mixing the hard infrastructure – research universities, research buildings, and telecommunications systems – with the soft infrastructure – entrepreneurs, professors, angel investors, venture capitalists, lawyers, accountants, consultants and other service providers. Even today, I'm frequently asked by entrepreneurs and government officials in Europe, Japan and Asia how they can create their own Silicon Valley.

What most people misunderstand is that the historical, cultural and social ecosystem of Silicon Valley is difficult, if not impossible to replicate. Silicon Valley is the latest Gold Rush in a long series of California gold rushes, beginning with the Spanish rancheros, the 1849 Gold Rush, the post-WW2 boom and the U.S.-Soviet space race. Since the beginning, California has seen wave after wave of immigrants who brought an open mind, fresh ideas and entrepreneurial energy. Silicon Valley is an open, dynamic society where people are free to pursue their dreams, unfettered by the heavy hand of family, traditions, authoritarian governments, and religious strife. Although "glass ceilings" still exist for women and minorities, Silicon Valley is more open to people who move about, reinvent themselves and test their ideas. Being different or unusual is not a showstopper. The major barrier is attitudinal. Silicon Valley is a mindset, not just a place, although the dynamic entrepreneurial ecosystem helps immensely. It is the endless drive, focus and resilience of Silicon Valley entrepreneurs who are attracted to solving big problems and willing to fail repeatedly to find solutions. In most places, late bloomers and failed entrepreneurs are not given a chance, let alone a second or third chance, so it isn't surprising that many entrepreneurs head to Silicon Valley to pursue their dreams. As Steve Jobs' advice -- "Stay hungry. Stay foolish." – is embraced in very few places in the world.

Many cities and regions have tried to build their own Silicon Valleys with mixed success. During the 1980s, Holland, Scotland, Ireland and Taiwan were the most successful, attracting hundreds of high-tech companies. The Netherlands Foreign Investment Agency and the Scottish Development Agency were the most polished. They hired high-tech business and financial managers who ran their operations like Intel and Apple Computer, spared no money in recruiting and training the top people, and aggressively courting Dataquest's clients at our conferences. Ireland copied them, creating the "Silicon Tiger" of the 1990s, followed by Scotland and Wales.

Wales was the most savvy. It held an annual golf tournament, inviting Japanese manufacturers to team up with Welsh high-tech managers in mixed pairs in a round of golf, followed by a banquet with Welsh dancing and music. Japanese managers sported beards, pipes, and Welsh accents. For them, Wales was paradise since they could play golf every day after work. Wales' campaign worked wonders; during the 1980s, Wales attracted over 10,000 local manufacturing jobs at Japanese companies.

Taiwan was the most driven Asian country in Silicon Valley, where its office name did not mention Taiwan for political reasons. Taiwan officials visited our Dataquest office frequently and grilled us about Silicon Valley and Japan, the semiconductor industry and PC market trends. We advised their organizing teams at the Electronics Research & Service Organization (ERSO) and the Institute for Technology Research (ITRI), which were in charge of developing the Hsinchu Science Park.

During the 1980s, the PC boom created a huge market for circuit boards, which Taiwanese contract manufacturers leaped on with passion. I still remember one Dataquest conference in 1985 when I pointed out a market hole between the desktop PC and the handheld device, and described a computer about the size of a notebook. Earlier, Alan Kay at Apple Computer had developed the DynaBook concept, but PC makers were focused on desktops at the time. Taiwanese researchers immediately grilled me about the notebook computer, which I felt was the next, inevitable step in personal computing. They were hungry for the next new thing. At trade shows, they would gather product brochures, lay them out in their executive suites and rearrange ideas to reverse-engineer products right on the spot, which would appear in the market within months.

One surprise was Singapore, which invited me to train students at the National Computing Institute in entrepreneurship. I found the idea an oxymoron since Singapore's repressive government had successfully created a generation of conformist students. For several days, I trained two dozen, well-mannered students who reminded me of Japanese students. Unlike Silicon Valley, the students only asked a few polite questions so I left feeling rather disappointed that I had failed. A few years later, to my surprise, I met two of my students who had started their ventures after taking my class – the first Singaporean entrepreneurs I had ever met – so there is hope in training young people in conservative environments. Now, Singapore is making a major effort to move up the innovation ladder by training entrepreneurs, but they still have a long way to go to overcome their socially engineered society.

But despite all these government efforts, few regions have been able to create the dynamism of Silicon Valley's entrepreneurial churn. They will continue to try with mixed results, but the attraction, weather and magic of the valley is still hard to beat.

Never underestimate the power of inspiration and ideas. Hungry, open-minded people will take your ideas and often run with them. The key is to learn from them in order to remain competitive and stay in touch with global markets.

Training China's Leaders

My first encounter with China came without warning.
In 1983, my Dataquest boss Gene Norrett advised me to
study Mandarin, saying, "the end of the 20th century
belongs to Japan, but the first half of the 21st century will
belong to China." I didn't study Mandarin since we
were so involved with Japan and the Four Tigers, but his
words came true four years later. I was invited by the
World Bank to lecture to fifty of China's top leaders –
ministry heads and vice mayors of Beijing, Shanghai and
other cities – who were studying the electronics industry
under a $2 million grant from the World Bank.

I remember my unease looking into a face of fifty serious,
older men dressed in somber suits. All afternoon, I
lectured about the Japanese and Asian electronics
industries, answering polite questions through an
interpreter. They knew very little about the electronics
industry so they ask rather basic questions about
Japanese, Asian and Silicon Valley high-tech
technologies, companies, industry dynamics, and
business practices. One topic that amused me was their
answer to my question about the potential size of the PC
market in China, which everyone in Silicon Valley was
salivating over. They looked puzzled as if they didn't
understand my question, so I asked again: How many
people buy PCs every year in China and what is the
project demand in five years?

One manager raised his hand and said: "Your question makes no sense to us. China produces very few computers every year, they break down after a few years, and we have a billion people. At our current rate of production, it will take decades to meet their needs, so demand has no meaning to us for now. We're only focused on producing as fast as we can." I couldn't help but laugh. PC makers around the world would love to have their problem – huge demand and limited supply in a closed market.

Although they were "economic lambs," they struck me as hardened political veterans. When I asked how many of them had participated in Mao's Long March, half of the hands went up. Fifty-two years earlier, during the last of the Long Marches in 1935, they were in their late teens or early twenties and had evaded the strong Kuomingtang forces. I asked what it was like. Several said they were scared for their lives since they didn't know if the farmers would support or attack them, but to their relief, the farmers gave them food and shelter, encouraging them in their fight against the Kuomingtang and eventually the Japanese army.

Everything went smoothly until the session ended at five o'clock. The group leader came up to me and asked where the banquet – a traditional custom in China for welcoming leaders – would be held. I asked the World Bank program manager, but he replied no banquet was planned and the group was free to go out on their own that evening. The Chinese group leader was visibly disappointed. "But the White House and Congress are right over there," he said, pointing out the window. "Don't we get to meet the President and your leaders? This is our first time in Washington D.C." The World Bank leader shook his head, hurriedly excused himself, saying he had to go home to his family, leaving me all alone, unassisted, with the fifty Chinese leaders and their interpreter. I couldn't believe it; the top fifty leaders of China on their first official visit to Washington D.C. and not one American political leader was here to greet them! Quickly, I bowed deeply and apologized on behalf of the United States for this incredibly embarrassing and rude breach of etiquette.

Visibly disappointed, the group leader broke the tension. "We miss Chinese food. Do you know any good Chinese restaurants around here?" I took them to a nice restaurant downtown. I remember the manager coming out to greet us, not believing me when I said this group, which had not called in a reservation, came from mainland China. He spoke to the Chinese leader, who pointed to his colleagues and politely asked for a banquet room. When the restaurant manager realized was the first group of Chinese leaders he had ever met, his eyes opened wide in total shock. He bowed deeply, scurrying out to get his entire staff, who bowed deeply as if Mao himself had walked in the door.

Escorted to the banquet room, the group leader
indicated that I would sit in the middle next to the
interpreter, surrounded by his team. "Let's be informal.
You can ask us any question you want. We want to
know more about America and Japan." So for the next
three hours, I had the rare and unimaginable privilege of
having a dinner with China's top leaders all by myself. I
still remember their faces beaming when the food was
served and we launched into an interesting discussion.
They asked me all sorts of questions about America,
Japan, Asia and Europe since this was their first trip
abroad. Why did Americans drive cars so much? What
television programs were popular? What did Americans
and Japanese think of China? How do Silicon Valley
companies operate? Would they want to do business with
China? How are startups created and run? Would they
want to partner with Chinese companies? How is
intellectual property handled in America? What should
China do to build its high-tech industries? How could
the U.S., Japan and Europe be involved? They also
wanted to know about my Japanese grandparents'
history and the detention of Japanese Americans in
camps during World War II.

In return, I asked them all sorts of questions about
Chinese cities, businesses, families and society since I had
never met mainland Chinese before. We were like
children asking each other basic questions about each
other's lives. They were incredibly curious, friendly and
driven, something that I've observed about Chinese

students and businessmen visiting the U.S. during the past few decades.

I had to ask one burning question: "What did they consider the biggest challenge facing China?" The leader said: "The one-child policy. All of our kids are turning into spoiled little princes and princesses. They get whatever they want. What will happen when they grow up?" I said I had one daughter, my little princess, so we all had a good laugh.

Spending nine hours alone with China's top leaders was definitely one of the most memorable experiences I've ever had. They were mostly engineers and hardened political veterans who were naïve about western economics, but very eager to learn. They reminded me of Japanese and Asian semiconductor executives – dedicated, serious, focused, and friendly. We exchanged business cards and they invited me to visit them, something that business people, politicians and China experts would long for. That evening, as their bus pulled away from the restaurant, I came away thinking that, with leaders like this, China had a very bright future indeed. They were serious about learning about our successes and failures. I had done my little part to connect with China and help them to create jobs. Little did I realize that within one decade China's electronic industry would emerge as a major player on the world stage and challenge the West.

Sometimes mistakes give you a glimpse into the future. Enjoy the opportunity, for it may never come again.

Fairchild Buyout

The big test of "Japanophobia" came in 1987 when
Fairchild Semiconductor, the first semiconductor
company and icon of Silicon Valley, was almost acquired
by the Japanese. The event triggered a huge outpouring
of self-scrutiny in Silicon Valley. Did we have a future?
Would our semiconductor industry survive? Intel had
just shut down its memory chip plants and was
refocusing on microprocessors; its future was still
uncertain. AMD and National Semiconductor, two
memory chip icons, were struggling to reposition
themselves. The U.S. Trade Commission had levied
anti-dumping tariffs on the Japanese memory
chipmakers, which were gloating with pride. I remember
visiting Japanese semiconductor managers in Tokyo who
lectured me about the "American sickness," which they
believed was terminal like the "British disease." Proud
and arrogant, they believed that Japan would dominate
the 21st century. At the time, with American chipmakers
struggling before the Japanese onslaught, Silicon Valley's
future seemed dark indeed. But I also knew that in
hubris and arrogance lay the seeds of failure. Japan
might be peaking. How long could it continue before it
slowed down or crashed?

So at the height of Japan's ascendency, I wasn't surprised
when my client and friend, Mark Shepard, called to tell
me that Fairchild Semiconductor, a Silicon Valley icon

and the training ground for the founders of Intel, AMD, National Semiconductor, and other leading chipmakers, was going to be acquired. I asked who it was, but Mark kept mum. "You guys (at Dataquest) figure it out," he said.

Taking his hint, I arranged for a dozen Dataquest top analysts to analyze Fairchild and identify who might be the ideal buyer. After much discussion and data analysis, we arrived at our conclusion, which I reported to Mark: Fujitsu, Hitachi and National Semiconductor, in that order. Mark wouldn't deny or confirm, but I wanted to see if his voice would give him away. Nothing.

"The Pentagon will never let you get away with it," I told him. "Fairchild has a Cray supercomputer in Milpitas (a town near San Jose) that the Pentagon will never let it be acquired by the Japanese, especially Fujitsu and Hitachi, which have competing supercomputer divisions. The Pentagon will never let the Japanese compromise our nuclear secrets, especially after Toshiba allowed propeller secrets to leak to the Soviet Union. Frankly, I'm disappointed that Fujitsu or Hitachi would even consider compromising the U.S. nuclear umbrella that protects Japan. Their CEO should have immediately rejected the idea."

Greg remained silent the entire time, but I knew I was right, especially since I was advising the Office of Technology Assessment (OTA) and Defense Analysis Institute (DIA) in Washington D.C., which were extremely worried about Japan's "leaky bucket." The Soviet Union had still not collapsed so the Cold War during the Reagan Administration was still tense. The United States could not afford to let the Soviets get hold of our supercomputing capabilities, which were on the export control list, via Japan. The stakes were incredibly high and I felt a patriotic duty to make sure American companies did nothing to compromise our nuclear security.

As Dataquest predicted, Fujitsu announced that it had offered to buy Fairchild. The press went wild over another example of the "Japanese buyout of America." Fairchild was called before Pentagon officials to justify the deal. Day after day, reporters called Dataquest for comments about the buyout. I reiterated the same line: the Pentagon will never let Fujitsu buy Fairchild because of its Cray supercomputer. The OTA kept asking Dataquest for insights about the buyout.

Needless to say, the Pentagon nixed the buyout and instructed Fairchild to sell to an American buyer, which it did. National Semiconductor announced it would buy Fairchild; the deal was consummated in 1987.

After the acquisition, I met Mark Shepard and asked him what had happened during the past year. He said it was a nightmare of legal paperwork, nearly a room full of documents, and constant meetings with Pentagon officials, which cost Fairchild over a million dollars in legal fees and thousands of hours of administrative time and endless meetings among its top managers and board members. He admitted that Dataquest's assessment had been correct. Fujitsu was the top bid, followed by Hitachi and National Semiconductor, in the order we predicted. I told Mark that Fairchild could have saved itself a million dollars by just paying Dataquest consulting fees to choose the appropriate buyer -- National Semiconductor – a year of time and money, and its reputation, along those of Fujitsu and Hitachi, if it had listened to people less focused on short-term financial gains and more on long-term strategic issues.

National security is nothing to be left to the whims of corporate dealmakers. The world is a dangerous place so they should always think through the implications of their deals thoroughly beforehand. It's cheaper than rushing deals.

NTT International

Japan is a tough market to crack for most foreigners because of the language and cultural barriers, strong cross-ownerships and closed society. Fortunately, my ability to speak and read Japanese, experience of teaching and working in Japan, and network of Japanese friends and relatives has made it easier for me to do business in Japan, but it's still a challenge. I tell Japanese that I'm an American who happens to speak, read and understand Japanese and has Japanese relatives, but am not a Japanese native or citizen. That puzzles most Japanese since I discuss most topics freely in Japanese. However, many assume that I was born in Japan and moved to America as a teenager or college student since I don't know all the latest lingo and developments in Tokyo.

Japanese treat me differently from other Americans and expect me to behave like a Japanese so I'm always careful to use polite Japanese with clients. This carefulness is especially important in dealing with Japanese companies who wield a great deal of economic clout internationally. My Dataquest boss, Fred Zieber, who had many friends in the Japan, advised me to welcome the Japanese in order to overcome the cultural barriers. "Roll out the red carpet to Silicon Valley. The warmer the welcome, the faster the doors will fly open in Japan." This advice is true with other nations too.

His advice was tested when the Dataquest Japan manager notified us that the CEO of NTT International, Japan's telecommunications conglomerate, wanted to visit Dataquest in San Jose and get a briefing on the latest trends. Wanting to make a good impression, I went around to Dataquest managers to invite them to speak half an hour each on market trends in their field. Almost all of them refused, saying they were too busy and NTT wasn't their client. Recalling Fred's advice, I cajoled them and finally got them to grudgingly agree to make presentations. I invited Manny Fernandez, our CEO, to have lunch with the Ohara-san, visiting NTT executive, advising him to just smile and answer any questions. The stage was set.

The Dataquest presentations went well and Manny had a pleasant lunch with the NTT executive. To my surprise, the CEO and I discovered that he had grown up in downtown Okayama City right around the block from where I lived during my two years as an English teacher through the San Jose-Okayama Sister City exchange program in the mid-1970s. My lodging house, a traditional building with tatami rooms and a common *ofuro* bathtub, had been a *ryokan*, a high-end guest lodge. We immediately felt a strong bond and talked about our neighborhood like pals. Delighted, he invited me to lunch when I visited Tokyo.

After he returned to Tokyo, the Dataquest Japan sales manager called to ask what we had done. I was afraid we had offended NTT in some way. The Dataquest manager said: "He thinks Dataquest is the greatest company in Silicon Valley." I replied: "We are. We walk on water."

Six months later, I had plans to visit Tokyo and notified the Dataquest Japan office to call NTT International and tell Ohara-san that I would like to have lunch with him. The Japan staff chuckled, saying that Ohara-san's invitation was a mere formality, not an actual invitation, and that a young person like me would never get invited to lunch by such a high-ranking in status-conscious Japan. Despite their skepticism, I asked them to call NTT. To their surprise, Ohara-san's secretary booked lunch with me, saying Ohara-san would come to the Dataquest Japan office to pick me up.

I'll never forget the expressions on the faces of the dozen Dataquest Japan employees when Ohara-san walked into the lobby. They jumped to attention and bowed deeply with respect, as if a warlord had walked into the room. Ohara-san smiled and came up to shake hands with me, saying: "Tatsuno-san lived in my neighborhood in Okayama." The Dataquest Japan staff were totally stunned and bowed deeply as we left. Graciously, he took me out to a wonderful sushi dinner in nearby Ginza, where we enjoyed chatting all evening with the sushi chef, totally immersed in sushi, beer and sake, a night I'll never forget. Ah, Tokyo at its best!

And the best surprise: Ohara-san ordered eleven Dataquest service subscriptions at $15,000 a piece, which made our half-morning presentations worth $165,000 in 1990 dollars, not a bad payback for our time and effort. But more importantly, Dataquest built strong ties with NTT International and had a good friend in Ohara-san, who recommended us to other Japanese companies.

Always roll out the red carpet in business, especially to foreigners, and doors will fly open faster.

1990s: The End of the Cold War

The fall of the Berlin Wall and collapse of the Soviet
Union sent California and other regions heavily
dependent upon Pentagon funding into a deep recession.
Military contractors laid off a quarter million workers in
California and an equal number on the East Coast.
Silicon Valley went into another funk, but this time
deeper and more worrisome than previous downturns.
The unemployment rate passed 12 percent. Worried
friends and colleagues asked me: Is there a future for
Silicon Valley? Should we stay or move and find new
careers? There were no new technologies in sight. The
future looked grim, with tens of thousands of engineers
leaving the field. The Department of Commerce held
military technology commercialization workshops up
and down the state, where I met desperate laid-off
workers and anxious entrepreneurs. One CAD
(computer aided design) company that had designed
military planes and vehicles switched to selling modified
designs on CD-ROMs to Hollywood for its war movies,
but it was the exception, a bright spot in an otherwise
barren economy. Most companies relying on the
Pentagon went bankrupt, throwing thousands of people
onto the streets. It was a time of desperation and a
scramble for new ideas. People searched high and low
for new business ideas and industries, but nothing was on
the immediate horizon. Silicon Valley was going under –

again – and only innovation would save its skin. But nobody had a clue where the future lay or, as many pessimists believed, if Silicon Valley had a future at all. By sheer luck, Apple Computer hired me as a consultant to help its strategy team redefine Apple's future, which was struggling with its aging Mac operating system (OS). It was a session I would never forget.

After the Berlin Wall collapsed, my friend Ken Lim, who worked with me at Dataquest and was working in the business strategy team at Apple Computer, invited me to participate in a one-day strategy planning workshop at Apple, which was ordered by then CEO John Sculley to review Apple's businesses and reposition for the future. Six other consultants were invited, including digital guru Howard Rheingold and a young guy from the East Coast named Steven Case. Seated in Apple's headquarters, we were told that Sculley wanted answers to two key questions: What should Apple do with its existing businesses? What new businesses it should consider? All of us consultants unanimously agreed that Apple should license the Mac OS since it hadn't improve much for six years so Microsoft's Windows had caught up with it. The strategy team said Sculley would not license the Mac OS and actually believed Apple's main competitor was NEC of Japan, not Microsoft, which totally stunned us because Sculley totally misunderstood Apple's positioning. Apple integrated software with hardware; it wasn't just another hardware company like NEC, which licensed the Microsoft Windows OS and bought commodity parts. Moreover, Microsoft was grabbing market share from Apple so we wondered why Sculley didn't see the growing threat. He wasn't a tech guy, but still he had a top tech team so his blindness worried us. No wonder Apple was going downhill; under that type of leadership, we feared for its very future.

To answer Sculley's second question, the strategy team put up butcher paper around the room and had us brainstorm the future of Apple. We dreamed up new businesses in education, consumer, and industrial markets. During the brainstorming, Steven Case stepped forward and totally dominated the session with his brilliance. He drew a huge graphic of the "multimedia marketplace of the future," which showed all sorts of new consumer online services like chat, shopping, music, etc. I was stunned by his visionary thinking and marketing brilliance, which reminded me of another brilliant entrepreneur whom I had met earlier – Michael Dell. The hair went up on the back on my neck listening to Steve, just as it had done when I had spoken with Michael.

I asked Dave Nagel, Apple's research manager, about Steve's background. He replied: "Steve's from Honolulu and ran a pizza shop back East. We invited him because the word on the street is that he's is a marketing genius. He just launched a new consumer service called America Online, which has about 9,000 subscribers."

Dave explained that Apple was launching a rival online service called eWorld, so Sculley wanted his eWorld strategy team to see firsthand how Steve thought; he basically wanted to pick Steve's brains without his knowledge. I was appalled but remembered that Steve Jobs had gotten the idea for the Mac from Xerox PARC. So I shook my head. All's fair in love and business -- and this was a behind-the-scenes war.

During the afternoon, we watched as Steve developed and defended his case for the online multimedia marketplace. He was brilliant, but I doubted that he could beat MCI, which had 1.2 million subscribers, IBM's new $1 billion online service, and Apple's upcoming eWorld service into which Sculley was planning to invest tens of millions of dollars. On the other hand, Steve was – as Sculley had correctly sized him up – "dangerous" so we all expected him to unveil a brilliant AOL marketing campaign in the future. What it was we had no clue, but I left convinced that Steve would succeed like Michael Dell.

Steve and Michael were by far the most brilliant entrepreneurs I had ever met and I had met hundreds of brilliant startup founders while working in Silicon Valley. These rare geniuses are like forces of nature; they have animal spirits and enormous focus, drive and stamina. They are unstoppable. They can be slowed and forced to retreat, but not easily defeated. They always find ways around obstacles. Whereas most smart people are great at analyzing dozens of ways something cannot be done (i.e. can't do), these guys focused on new ways of getting things done.

Little did I know that Steve's real reason for coming to Apple was not just to earn some consulting dollars, but raise money from Apple's venture fund. Years later, I was chatting on the phone with my friend and former Dataquest colleague Gary Madden, who had run Apple's venture fund. When I said Sculley had blown it at Apple, Gary said with a deep sigh: "Yeah, really big time." Suspecting a bigger story, I asked what he meant.

"Remember the day you and Steve worked for Apple as consultants? I approved Steve's request for a $2 million investment from our fund, but Sculley refused to approve it, despite urging from the entire Apple strategy team. Sculley said he would crush the kid, even though we all knew he was dangerous. Apple spent $2 million every month on coffee and other luxuries. We urged Sculley to hedge his bets, but he refused – not once, but four times. That was the biggest screw-up of all time. In 2000, AOL stock went through the roof and Apple would have owned a huge chunk of AOL. We could have financed Apple research to eternity and beyond. Sculley and I would have been famous and on every business magazine cover around the world."

I was totally stunned, shaking my head in total disbelief. Sculley's team and all of us consultants had seen that

Steve was a veritable business genius and, yet, Sculley had passed. The biggest pass in Silicon Valley history.

Never get too big for your britches. Often the kids will show you up. In fact, most of the breakthrough high-tech startups of all time have been founded by twenty-somethings --- Dell, AOL, Yahoo!, eBay, Google, Facebook, etc. So take the risk. Bet on wild-eyed kids who don't know any better and don't care about the established ways of doing business. Once in a while they'll hit one out of the ballpark.

Intel Inside

Intel is an amazing company when it bothers to listen to its customers. In the spring of 1992, I first encountered the "new Intel" when my friend Barbara Holtzman called me to say that a friend at her synagogue, Avram Miller, Intel's new Vice President of Business Development, was planning to visit Japan and wanted to hire a Japanese speaker. Having had Intel as a client at Dataquest during the 1980s, I immediately jumped at the opportunity and met Avram, who surprised me with his casual elegance. Unlike the straitlaced Intel engineers and marketers whom I knew, Avram looked like a former hippie, with long, flowing hair, animated gestures and a grin on his glowing face. I was immediately charmed by his warmth and brilliance. He an accomplished pianist and sat on the board of a record company. One of the smartest guys I had met in Silicon Valley, Avram was musician to boot, which appealed to me since I had just begun screenwriting after having worked on two successful TV documentaries. We immediately hit it off.

My first question: Why in the world does Intel need a VP of Business Development since it had a virtual monopoly in the microprocessor market? Avram quipped "only the paranoid survive" – repeating the famous line by Intel co-founder Andy Grove. As I had witnessed in 1985, the Japanese memory chipmakers had nearly put Intel out of business so Intel's "troika" was rightfully paranoid about remaining competitive. Even with its market dominance, Intel could not afford to be complacent. The PC market was changing fast with the growth of Microsoft's Windows operating system.

But why Japan? Avram said the troika didn't like visiting Japan because of the bad memories engendered by its near bankruptcy at the hands of Japanese chipmakers. Most Japanese clients interpreted Intel's aloofness as arrogance; it was more a matter of pure fear and respect. After all, the Japanese chipmakers were trying to beat Intel in microprocessors with the government-sponsored TRON Project and their own chips. The troika feared a repeat of the memory chip debacle and didn't want its engineers leaking secrets to its Japanese competitors. Avram wanted to introduce himself and build bridges with Japanese customers, who were both friends and rivals. I nodded, but was not fully convinced of his explanation.

As I suspected, the real reason for our visit came out after we arrived in Tokyo. Over dinner, Avram bent over the table and quietly confided: "This is top secret. We're here to ask Intel customers three questions: Should Intel enter consumer markets? Should Intel advertise? And should we build one product per plant? We can't ask these questions in the U.S. or Wall Street would hammer our stock since consumer markets mean low profit margins. That's why we're in Japan. These guys understand consumer markets and we're far enough away from headquarters."

I understood why Intel wanted to hear what the Japanese thought about the first two questions, but the third question totally puzzled me. Why only run one product per plant? Avram explained that when Intel built a $1 billion plant, it took six to nine months to break even. After that, its margins approached 90%, which turned each plant into a virtual printing press of money. But product changes were a big problem.

"When we change products in a factory, it takes about two months to install and test the equipment for the new products. Each switch costs about $150 million to $200 million. If the plant was already paid off, why switch to a new product and lose money while the plant is shut down? Why not just run it full out? Even if we lowered prices, we would still be wildly profitable."

"Because the product would age and become a commodity," I replied. "You could cut prices drastically and end up competing directly with AMD at the low end."

"Exactly. That's why we're here in Japan. Consumer is 35% of all semiconductor use in Japan so I want to hear directly from Japanese customers. But we won't tell them why we're here. I'll just slip in the three questions throughout our get-acquainted meetings and hope they don't catch onto our goals."

Avram broke into a broad grim like a Cheshire cat, which he would do many times during the next few weeks as we visited a dozen Japanese customers, including NEC, Fujitsu, Hitachi, Toshiba, IBM Japan, Matsushita, Mitsubishi, Sega, and Nintendo. During each meeting, Avram casually asked the three questions and the Japanese invariably replied: "But Intel started in consumer markets with Busicom in 1974. Why did you ever leave? And can you sell us a consumer microprocessor for $25, not $250 like now?"

But I remember NEC, Toshiba, and Mitsubishi managers asking whether Intel could give them labels indicating that there was an Intel processor inside their PC. They offered to stick the Intel label onto the computers in the factories. Avram asked why they wanted the label. All three managers said: "Nobody knows our PCs overseas, but if they see we use Intel processors, then they'll know the PC works. If we sell more PCs, you'll sell more chips to us."

Avram and I looked at each quizzically, the first time we had ever heard such a strange request. I imagined a glittery children's sticker, but the managers said they wanted something like the Underwriters Laboratory (UL) label. It made sense; the more PCs they sold, the more processors Intel would sell to them. Avram took their requests back to headquarters.

About nine months later, Intel unveiled the "Intel Inside" marketing campaign, which became one of the most successful marketing campaigns in Silicon Valley history. NEC, Toshiba and Mitsubishi were among the first to put the Intel label onto their PCs. I was stunned that Intel moved so fast in making such a dramatic shift from business into consumer markets after we visited Japan. That was one of the boldest moves in the valley's history since it affected the bottom line and dramatically changed its business model.

Another surprising move: Avram's Business Development team later became Intel Capital, which invested $1 billion and reportedly made $4 billion in the late 1990s, so I was unofficially the first member of Intel Capital as a consultant.

Marketing in Silicon Valley fundamentally changed after "Intel Inside", forcing chipmakers to advertise themselves more aggressively. After "Intel Inside," Silicon Valley made a rapid shift from business PC users to the faster-growing consumer PC market.

Years later, I was chatting with my good friend Steve Yamaguma, a local graphic designer, about the Intel Inside campaign. Steve said that earlier, in 1991, he had been contracted by Intel to develop a marketing label. He came up with a label that said something like "There's an Intel processor inside," but for some reason, the marketing campaign was halted and the entire team disbanded. I suspect that they were either fired or reassigned since "consumers" were a dirty word at Intel at the time. That's why Avram wanted us to test his marketing ideas in Japan – to avoid the overwhelming fear of thin consumer profit margins in Silicon Valley and on Wall Street.

Customers often make strange, inconvenient requests, but pay attention and listen carefully. Often they're onto something much bigger than your best teams can possibly imagine.

Stanford University and the Mosaic browser

Life has a way of catching one totally by surprise. When times are tough, magical doors can suddenly fly open. My father, deeply spiritual Christian layman, often said: "God works in mysterious ways, his wonders to perform." But in 1993, with the United States in a serious recession after the end of the Cold War, it was hard to remain optimistic. My wife was diagnosed with a failing liver and my consulting business was falling off a cliff. It was not a good time to be an independent consultant.

Miraculously, my former Dataquest client at Hewlett-Packard, Dr. Robert Burmeister, had been hired by Stanford's electrical engineering department to run a new U.S.-Japan Technology Management Center (USJTMC), which had been established by Congress to train engineering and computer science at eight U.S. universities in Japanese technical language and business practices. He offered me a job -- a godsend during the tough downturn – as Industry Liaison Manager to involve Silicon Valley and Japanese companies into Stanford's engineering programs. Despite its reputation for close industry-business ties, Stanford emphasizes theory and its professors are so busy teaching and researching that they often lack the time to pursue business collaboration. That has changed substantially today, but in 1993, few Stanford researchers knew much about Japanese technologies and business practices, which was the reason for establishing the center. Moreover, many engineering students wanted real-world business knowledge since most of them end up in business, not academia, so I was a conduit. I knew hundreds of Silicon Valley companies so it was easy for me to involve them.

Although the job required a long commute from the Santa Cruz, I eagerly accepted the job since I wanted to work at Stanford part-time to see how the university operated and enjoy the intellectual stimulation of Stanford faculty and students, as I had done with Professor Daniel Okimoto at the Asia Pacific Research Center during the 1980s while I worked at Dataquest.

Settled into the aging McCullough building that smelled of gases from labs, I asked the program student interns how to send email and surf the Internet. One of the students replied: "Learn Unix." Since I'm a business guy who doesn't write computer programs, I asked them: "Can you guys develop a Mac interface for the Internet so I can send email and search without having to learn Unix? It should be simple so I only have to click buttons and icons."

The students looked at me incredulously, saying: "Just learn Unix. It's easy. They offer classes."

I told them the National Science Foundation had just announced it would no longer subsidize the Internet, but let it be commercialized as a way to fund its expansion. I said that was huge news, as epic making as the invention of the transistor, and that everyone would soon be using the Internet, including businesses, schools and families, to work, study, play, and communicate.

"I have a 65-year-old aunt in Illinois," one of the students. "What would she do on the Internet?" "Shop," I replied. "But there's nothing to buy on the Internet," he argued.

I told him that people would soon buy anything they wanted since retailers would come pouring onto the Internet, but he disagreed, saying there was no way to pay.

"Programmers will figure out an online payment method," I replied. "There are thousands of programmers who could do it."

"Even if they do, people won't trust the Internet."

"Someday, we'll be buying anything you can imagine."

"Anything? We'll never buy cars or houses online. They're too big and expensive."

I recoiled in total disbelief, saying size or price would be irrelevant on the Internet, which would eventually sell everything, large or small. He remained skeptical, saying: "We're not going to bastardize the Internet so my aunt can shop online."

I was stunned by his arrogance; he thought the Internet would always remain the province of elite researchers, even though it was common knowledge that most Silicon Valley technologies begin at DARPA, universities and NASA, then are commercialized for enterprise markets before going into consumer markets. I told him everyone would use it so we should develop a simple interface for the Internet, but they said they were too busy and walked off – the biggest mistake in Silicon Valley history!

During the next few months, I asked other Stanford students and researchers to help me develop an Internet interface. I attended Don Norman's course on next-generation computer-human interfaces, which attracted a hundred of Silicon Valley's smartest software programmers from Stanford and local companies, but nobody would help me. When they discovered that I wasn't a programmer, they just smiled and walked away. My idea was too simple, not worthy of the elegant software algorithms they were discussing in class. Out of pure frustration, I finally enrolled in Stanford's Unix classes and learned the basics.

During the fall of 1993, there was much discussion about the upcoming commercial Internet, but all discussions focused on technical issues like RSA security protocols. I felt that it was like discussing the type of locks one would install on a business, which were needed, but begged the bigger questions: What kind of businesses would emerge on the Internet? How would people use it? How would they market and sell products and services? How would they handle payment? Nobody was asking those questions, not even Stanford Business School. Stanford's engineering focus was overshadowing its business and social awareness. Nobody was thinking about the average user like me.

Today, Internet businesses are common sense even to the average child, but at the time it was not very obvious since there were no precedents. Trying to predict the future was useless. Even though Alan Kay of Apple Computer said "the best way to predict the future is to invent it," it wasn't obvious how to invent Internet businesses. In hindsight, the only way to predict the future was to ask questions, then build it. How would one sell books online? Amazon! How would one run auctions online? Ebay! How would one sell airline tickets online?   Expedia and Travelocity! But nobody at Stanford was asking those questions at the time, just discussing technical issues.

I'll never forget the day in December when one of the interns walked into my office and dropped a floppy disc onto my desk. "What is it?" I asked. "Mosaic," he replied. "It's a browser." "What's that?" I asked. "Remember the Mac interface for the Internet? You got it," he replied. "You finally did it?" I asked. "No, some kid named Marc Andreesen at the University of Illinois wrote it," he replied.

"They beat us! And we had an eight-month lead! We would have been famous!"

"What are you all excited about?" he asked. "It's just a browser."

"Do you realize what just happened?" I said. "Now, everybody, including kids, will be using the Internet. All hell will break loose soon! We would have been famous, one of most successful inventors in Silicon Valley history! We blew it! We would have launched the Internet into businesses and homes!"

The intern shook his head, wondering what I was getting all excited about. My heart sank. Illinois had beaten Stanford! Here, we were in bastion of Silicon Valley, the biggest concentration of savvy programmers and interface designers in the world, and a student at the University of Illinois had beaten us! Mosaic was renamed Netscape and became the biggest IPO (initial public offering) in Silicon Valley history, which set off the Internet boom. We missed the opportunity of a lifetime! We would have become poster boys for Silicon Valley, but gave it away to a kid from Illinois. I should have looked outside of Stanford and found a high school kid to do the programming, but didn't.

If you want something, find people who share your vision and build it. Don't wait or others will beat you to the punch.

Yahoo!

Although I missed becoming the Mosaic co-developer, I was one of its first users at Stanford. When I first uploaded it to my Mac, I was awed by the ease with which I could surf the Internet. I was happier than a clam. But after a few weeks, I got irritated because there was no way to save Internet sites in memory. One had to write down each domain name, which was time-consuming. And if you miswrote a single letter, slash or dot, you couldn't find the web site again. University and government research sites invariably had long domain names that stretched across the Mosaic bar so it seemed to take forever to write down, recheck each domain and not lose the piece of paper with the list of domain names.

Complaining to one of the US-Japan Tech Management Center interns, I said Mosaic erred by not providing a way to save domain names. One of the interns gestured for me to come to the window. Looking out from our office, he pointed to a small trailer parked across the alleyway from McCullough Hall where we were working, saying:

"Two of my dorm buddies – Jerry Yang and David Filo – are doing exactly what you want. Their solution is called bookmarks. Just go to their Yahoo site to download it."

I was pleased to hear about the solution, but wondered what Jerry and David were doing working and living in a trailer.

The students said: "They're crazy. They're dropping out of the PhD program to run the Yahoo site. Jerry worked at the campus library and is trying to categorize all web sites on the Internet." I was thunderstruck. What a brilliant idea! The student replied: "There's no technical brilliance required at all. A kid could do that. With a PhD, they could work anywhere in the world. Why waste your time building a free directory?"

I argued that business people and consumers using the Internet would get lost. The only way to find their way around was Yahoo! They had to go through Yahoo! It was the pass through the growing mountain of Internet sites. Jerry and David had foreseen that Internet users would get lost online and set up Yahoo as an easy-to use directory. How brilliant and simple! Now, people would be able to explore the Internet quickly and easily without having to remember and write down long domain names.

"If you think they're so great, why don't you join them?" said the student. "I can introduce you. We're all buddies in the dorm and play mahjong all the time. But they need help. Yahoo is getting kicked off the Stanford server because its traffic is crashing the campus system. Stanford told them to move off-campus and get their own server but Jerry and David can't even spell business.

You're a business guy so maybe you can help them write a business plan and raise angel money."

Unfortunately, my wife had just gotten a liver transplant at the University of California at San Francisco's medical center and I was driving over 150 miles per day from Santa Cruz to Stanford and, after work, to San Francisco, then back to Santa Cruz at night to be with my daughter. My back hurt and I didn't have any time, energy or money to help a raw startup company, so I didn't meet Jerry or David. Instead, I focused on organizing Stanford's first Japanese Internet conference and inviting industry leaders. Big mistake! I would have been Yahoo's third employee, its first "suit."

Always walk across the street and kick the tires! You never know if the kids across the street are starting the next Yahoo!

But in hindsight, I have no regrets. For me, family comes first and is more than money or fame. I grew up in the Methodist Church and YMCA so I was raised to serve others. At YMCA camp, I carved a wooden plate inscribed with the motto "I'm Third" -- God first, others second, I'm third. Although I've often failed to heed this motto, I try hard to live it in my everyday life, even though it often means taking backseat, missing opportunities like Yahoo and letting others get all the fame, money and glory, which has happened many, many times during my life. But I would rather live with a clear conscience and be able to look at myself in the mirror in the morning, knowing that I had lived my life with love, integrity and honor. I always remember what a family friend once told me: What will you tell your daughter about your life at 80? Or, as the Native Americans say: Think of the seventh generation hence.

Perhaps a consolation came from a Silicon Valley attorney who confided that he advises entrepreneurs who strike it rich, especially famous founders, to move into gated communities, hire bodyguards for the family, and avoid traveling alone in Europe and other places. For someone who loves walking around cities, that would be like being imprisoned. Better to be average and walk freely than to be wealthy and trapped behind bars of wealth and security for life. For me, that would be a living death.

For me, genuine wealth in life is health, family, great friends, pursuit of your dreams and the freedom to travel and explore.

Needless to say, after Yahoo became popular, venture capitalists funded a dozen Internet directories within a few months in order to capitalize on the exploding Internet market. As I had predicted, e-commerce sites like Amazon and others came flooding onto the Internet, growing faster and bigger than I had ever imagined. I had predicted Internet sales of $1 billion in five years, which was laughable in 1993, but the Gartner Group said Internet sales had surpassed $45 billion. Later, friends asked why I was always so conservative in my forecast, but like my work with Bangalore ten year earlier, I never expected Internet commerce to grow so fast.

In late 1994, I left Stanford and returned to my Dreamscape Global consulting practice, which involved me with AMD Japan. One day, while I was working at home, I received a call from Randy Haykin, an Apple Computer sales rep who had graduated from Stanford Business School. He wanted to know what the future of Silicon Valley was. I told him the Internet. Then, he popped a question: "Have you ever heard of Yahoo?" Saying that I could have been Yahoo's third employee, he said that he had just gotten a job offer from Yahoo to be Vice President of Marketing. I asked if he was going to take it.

"That's the problem. They have no money and want me to raise it. But I need my Apple job because I have two kids, a mortgage and a big business school loan. I need a salary and the medical insurance."

I asked how long he could hold his breath financially if he quit Apple to join Yahoo. He said four months; his wife would move back with their kids to her parents if they went bankrupt.

The joys and dilemmas of living in Silicon Valley! Many entrepreneurs want to launch startups but need income to pay the bills. That's why most entrepreneurs work on their startup part-time at night and on weekends while holding down a regular job. It's another reason why many of the great tech startups – Dell, Apple, AOL, Yahoo!, eBay, and Google – are started by young people between 19 and 26. They can work around the clock at their startups because they don't have to worry about families, mortgages and kids. If they fail, and most do, they can get a regular job and try again, something that's hard for middle-aged people. Moreover, young people often don't know that they can't "achieve the impossible," but do it anyway because they use their creativity to bypass obstacles and solve problems. They're not burdened with legacy systems and old-fashioned thinking.

So Randy asked me what he should do. I told him: "Yahoo is white hot. Its traffic is going vertical. You'll only get this type of opportunity once in your lifetime. If I were you, I would quit Apple, help Yahoo raise money and don't look back." Randy was silent, then said: "Are you sure?" I replied: "I inherited intuition from my mom. My gut is never wrong. I can sense trends and events in advance. Yahoo is big and growing fast. It reminds me of Dell and AOL. Quit Apple and you'll never regret it."

Randy quit Apple and joined Yahoo, cashing out years later and becoming a venture capitalist who invested millions of dollars into his own portfolio of companies.

If you want to hit it big, you've got to take risks. When the opportunity comes, ask your friends. If they discourage you, but your gut tells you otherwise, go for it and don't look back.

Japan's Internet Future

Stanford is one of the most wonderful universities in the world because of its warm, collegial environment, high-caliber professors and students, and open-mindedness. But its relaxed resort environment belies its burning intensity. Professors, researchers and managers are pretty much free to do whatever they wanted, within ethical and legal limits of course, as long as they find funding. As many Stanford folks told me when I worked for the U.S.-Japan Technology Management Center (USJTMC) in the engineering department from 1993 to 1994: money talks, so find funding and you can run a program. That's why Stanford is so entrepreneurial; its people are always seeking funding for their research and programs, especially the engineering departments, which involve a fourth of the campus population. Think of the campus as Stanford Inc., a Fortune 1000 company with its departments serving as startup incubators, and you'll understand its dynamics.

At USJTMC, my boss Bob Burmeister was seeking a new technology that could attract funding. He focused on supercomputing, which had undergone tremendous growth during the Cold War due to the Pentagon's expanded nuclear bomb design and testing programs during the Reagan era. But with the collapse of the Soviet Union, funding for supercomputing was drying up, so universities and companies were scrambling for limited government funding and seeking new industrial applications. The U.S. Department of Commerce sponsored commercialization programs to help engineers shift from the downsizing military and aerospace industries to new commercial markets. Bob thought an industrial supercomputing program would attract top engineers, computer makers and industrial users to Stanford.

As a former Dataquest market researcher, I was rather skeptical about supercomputing, which I viewed as gold-plated machines because of their origin as nuclear bomb design and testing systems. Supercomputing and superconducting were big-ticket items that required heavy government spending and a lot of lobbying, but the federal government was cutting budgets. Moreover, faster, cheaper, more innovative supercomputers were being developed, but they hadn't found new non-military markets. They were caught in the classic "technology in search of a market" dilemma. Without urgent market demand, even the most innovative supercomputers would fail to sell and most supercomputer companies of that era did fail. Moreover, industrial supercomputing was such a small sector that I doubted it could absorb many of the 150,000-plus laid-off engineers in California quickly enough before their unemployment checks ran out. Silicon Valley needed a big, new industry – and fast. The only big new thing I saw coming that could absorb hundreds of thousands of engineers and programmers was the Internet. It was limited to military and university researchers, but I felt that would change soon.

In mid-1993, I had read a small article announcing that the National Science Foundation would no longer subsidize the Internet, which would go commercial in January 1994. I still remember the hair going up on the back of my neck. That's it, I thought – the Internet! The article reminded me of accounts of the 1947 article announcing the first transistor. I thought the Internet was the future of Silicon Valley since there would be millions of businesses and consumers using it in the near future. If our center jumped on the coming Internet boom, we would be famous. By early 1994, the Yahoo! site was already getting too many users, with Stanford's servers going down often, so I was convinced the Internet would boom.

I convinced Bob to let me organize one of Stanford's first Internet conferences in October 1994 by inviting fifteen Japanese networking experts from government, business and universities, including notables such as Internet guru Joichi Ito. The USJTMC interns, who were engineering and computer science students, jumped onto the new topic with enthusiasm since it was attracting so much attention and energy.

One day, a month before our conference, I got a call from a U.S. Army Intelligence manager in Fort Meade, Maryland, who asked if we had any conference seats available. He wanted to sign up six people and sounded very worried that he couldn't get them in. I asked him why. "My group runs the entire communications network for the Army, Air Force, and Navy in Japan, so we need to know what the Japanese are planning." I was dumbstruck. I knew U.S.-Japan relations were based on America's nuclear umbrella and that all armed force planning and maneuvers between the two nations and our allies were closely coordinated, but it never dawned on me that the commercial Internet would be so vital to the Pentagon's planning. I assumed they only worried about secure military communications networks.

However, it was becoming obvious that the Internet, which was originally developed by DARPA (Defense Advanced Research Projects Agency), the Pentagon's research funding arm, would have a much bigger impact on military planning and operations than I had anticipated. Even though I had worked at Bechtel Corporation's international project finance and planning teams during the late 1970s, where we did worst-case scenario "war gaming" to anticipate political, economic and military crises, I did not expect the Pentagon to be so worried about the commercial Internet. After all, it had been commercialized due to decisions at the National Science Foundation to offload the costs of maintaining the Internet to the business sector. In hindsight, I should have anticipated the prospect of "cyber wars" and "cyber-terrorism", but at the time few people outside of government agencies and universities understood the Internet or thought about the impacts it would have on civilian life, business and the military. Hackers were still unknown to most people. Outside of clandestine military networks, the Internet was still a technical phenomenon with no particular business or consumer relevance.

So, in October 1994, we held the first Japanese Internet conference, which was a complete success, attracting over 200 American, Japanese and Asian business managers and government officials, including six Army researchers from Fort Meade. Bob, the student interns and I were extremely pleased by the attendance. Our center had been funded by Congress and was being managed by Air Force Intelligence in Wright-Patterson Air Force Base in Ohio, so we were proud to be able to offer a valuable program. Although the Pentagon and NASA catalyzed the rise of Silicon Valley, few people realize that even today the Pentagon and Homeland Security provide enormous amounts of secret funding to Silicon Valley companies and universities to maintain military preparedness. Indeed, the U.S. government is still one of the biggest "venture capitalists" in town and is often the early funder of Silicon Valley's chips, computers, software, telecommunications and Internet startups. The CIA, for example, runs In-Q-Tel to fund "mission-impact technologies." Needless to say, foreign intelligence agencies routinely monitor Silicon Valley for both commercial and military technologies, which make the valley one gigantic cat-and-mouse labyrinth that the news media rarely cover in-depth. However, that is changing with the rise of Brazil, Russia, India and China – the BRIC nations – the Mideast and Asia. Although these regions are gaining economic clout, many of the leading technologies still come out of Silicon Valley.

Little did we realize at the time that we were sitting at the edge of one of the biggest technology booms in history. Like the transistor, the Internet came in quietly, apparent only to those who followed technology trends closely and recognized their relevance for commercial markets. It would totally change all of our lives and, ironically, it was an overlooked government-funded technology that was right under our noses.

Look carefully at government programs. Sometimes, you'll find new business, educational, cultural and nonprofit opportunities and industries overlooked by others.

Nokia's Global Launch

One of the joys of consulting is getting hired for the occasional surprise project. From 1994, Professor Gary Hamel of the London School of Business, who launched his strategy consultancy Strategos and grew it to $2 million in bookings in 18 months, and his Silicon Valley partner Linda Yates, invited me to work periodically as a subcontractor to help with their strategy training sessions at EDS, Whirlpool, Best Buy, Advanta and other major corporations. They had a superb team in London region and wanted a Silicon Valley expert who had advised top companies.

One day, Gary called to ask me to fly to Heathrow Airport in London to meet a new client, Nokia. I asked whether it was a Japanese company, but he said it was an old Finnish company that sold a variety of products. Its strategy team would tell me more. I was intrigued by Gary's rather sketchy description of the project, especially when he said: "This meeting never happened." I was puzzled; what did he mean by that? "Ultra top secret. Don't tell anyone, including your wife and friends. Nokia wants to hold its strategy planning session at Heathrow because everyone talks in Helsinki."

I caught a plane to Heathrow and found myself wandering around a warren of run-down buildings, totally lost. I couldn't find any grey-hair executives, only dozens of young people in jeans and open shirts who looked like college students at an academic retreat. After wandering around the complex, I finally asked one of the young women if she had seen a company called Nokia. "Oh, that's us," she replied. "We're in that room."

I was totally dumbstruck when I walked into the room to find about 60 to 70 young Nokia strategy people milling about, chatting, brainstorming, sketching on whiteboards, and joking about. It looked like a Silicon Valley startup, but filled with tall, then Finns. The woman introduced me to a young man who greeted me. "Welcome to Nokia. We're glad you can join us. We hear you're the Silicon Valley strategy guru." He led me to the group and introduced me. "Where is your leader?" I asked. "We really don't have a leader," was the reply. A woman pointed to an older fellow. "He's 31, the oldest one here, so I suppose he's our unofficial leader." The team ranged from 21 to 27 years of age. For many members, this was the first job out of college.

The Nokia team showed me their latest mobile phones, which were small, gleaming, smartly designed phones. I had never seen Nokia phones and I wanted to take one home.

"Nokia was founded over a hundred years old," explained one of the staff people. "The original company still makes rubber boots, chemicals, tires and other products. Recently, we spun out a new company to make digital cell phones based on technology that we licensed from the Finnish military. We've totally saturated the Finnish market, which only has 5 million people, and have entered northern Germany. The CEO wants to go global, but we lack the experience and knowledge. That's why we invited you."

Having advised over 500 high-tech companies while working at Dataquest and through my own consultancy, I knew how high-tech corporations developed their marketing and sales strategies. Usually, my clients suffered from flat or declining sales; some were literally "basket cases" in the midst of firing thousands of people and hired me in a last-ditch effort to turn around their businesses. I became know as a "turnaround doctor" because so many of my clients were in serious trouble. In Silicon Valley, over half of the companies regularly lose money so the turnaround market is large, but most CEOs and boards are in denial or too proud and would rather muddle through than hire outsiders to help them reconnect with their customers. Most are MBA graduates who know how to cut costs and fire people, but not how to find new markets and generate new sales.

Fortunately, Nokia's CEO and board made some smart strategic decisions. They spun off and incorporated the digital phone group as a new company so the existing bureaucracy would not drag it down. One of the young people said: "There are two Nokias. The Old Nokia is mostly socialists who sold to the Soviet Union. We're the New Nokia. We're mostly young capitalists who look to the West and Asia for our cell phone sales. You need to help us figure it out since almost none of us have any international marketing experience."

With that challenge tossed at me, I gave a presentation to the whole Nokia global launch team on how Nokia could become a global player, using examples from IBM, Intel, and other great Silicon Valley companies. The presentation went well and I was happy with the rapt attention paid by the young people. A few polite questions were asked, but then a young man stood up with a very serious look on his face. Everyone became absolutely quiet and the mood became very focused and intense. I knew it was a pivotal moment.

"You talk about Nokia becoming a successful company overseas, but no Finnish electronics company has ever gone global and became famous," he said. "Sweden has Ericcson and ABB, but we have absolutely nothing. Are we kidding ourselves? You've seen all the great companies in Silicon Valley and Japan. We're just a bunch of young people who've never gone international. Do you seriously think we have a chance to become a major global player or not?"

I clearly remember the question and the entire Nokia staff turning deathly silent and waiting for my reply. I felt extremely uncomfortable since my credibility was on the line. I was being challenged in front of everyone. Whatever I said would stick in their minds as long as they lived. My words would have huge impact on their young, impressionable minds and their ultimate global strategy.

Pausing for a long time, I finally answered: "Let me tell it to you straight. I'm from Silicon Valley where we don't take bullshit, but get to the point quickly. Do you want to hear what I frankly think about your chances for succeeding globally? I inherited intuition from my mother and I rarely miss." I looked around at all the young, beaming faces, which were anxiously waiting to hear my reply. I felt a heavy responsibility on my shoulders since I didn't want to deceive them by being polite. My reputation and credibility were riding on my answer and I couldn't get it wrong, not after Strategos said I was a strategy guru and I had set up their expectations with my reply.

"Frankly," I said. "As you're currently organized, I don't think you have a chance. You're like a college hockey team going against the Russians in the Olympic finals. You'll get killed in global competition." A big groan filled the room as all the young people looked dismayed, almost wanting to quit their strategy planning. But I wanted to give them hope and inspiration.

"If you want to be IBM, think like IBM. Find a recruiter and hire the smartest marketing manager in each market that you enter, train them on your technology in Helsinki, and listen very carefully to what they tell you and move fast. If you do that, you might have a chance."

I knew my advice was being carefully measured and weighed by everyone. Is this Silicon Valley guy bullshitting us or is his advice for real? I could feel my words sink into the group, which became very uneasy and restless, a mood that carried through the next three days I was with them. When I returned to Silicon Valley, I wondered if they would listen to my advice and even had a chance. Strategy consultants like me are regularly contracted to validate and reconfirm a company's thinking, which is often not possible to say or promote open within conservative organizations. We can say the unmentionable and offer drastic changes. If the company succeeds, the CEO and board usually take credit for the turnaround; if it fails, they can blame us consultants.

However, Nokia was no mood for corporate politics since Finland was undergoing a major transformation after the fall of the Soviet Union, which essentially killed its traditional product markets. So Nokia went out and hired the top marketing people around the world for their global expansion. I didn't pay much attention to their rollout since I was commuting regularly from Silicon Valley to Tokyo working on AMD Japan's and Canon's turnaround at the time, but three and half years later, I opened the business section in the San Jose Mercury and saw the headline that sent shock waves through Silicon Valley: Nokia beats Motorola to become #1 in the cell phone market. I was stunned. How did a young, inexperienced team beat the top player so quickly? Gary Hamel called to celebrate the good news: "We beat Motorola," he crowed. What a heady experience! A young Finnish team beating one of the top companies in the world. It was like the inexperienced U.S. ice hockey team beating the Russians at the 1980 Winter Olympics. Miracle with cell phones! We had beaten the odds.

Nokia has been one of the high points in my Silicon Valley career, very much like my experiences with Acer's U.S. launch, Applied Materials' entry into Japan, Intel's 1985 turnaround and "Intel Inside." As a consultant, I never made much money on these turnarounds, but it was fun being part of the winning teams. In Silicon Valley, it's those successes that offset the string of inevitable failures that drive us to do the impossible. We always want to work on the coolest projects doing the most amazing – or what Steve Jobs calls awesome – things. We love inventing the future when it's with the top teams in the world.

If you want to bet on the future, find driven young people with vision and a lot of energy. Today, they're likely to be found in the developing regions.

Missing the MP3 Player

I'm not a programmer or engineer, but one of the joys of being in Silicon Valley is spotting new technologies and working with creative technicalk people. In 1997, my former Dataquest colleague Tom Wang hired me to be Vice President of Business Development at Genoa Systems, a 3D graphics board vendor that enjoyed its heyday during the early 1990s. I'm not a game player, but thought the challenge would be an interesting change of pace from consulting. Tom wanted to diversify into new products since the 3D board market was becoming saturated. There were 47 graphics chip vendors, entering and exiting the business like a revolving door, and 3D graphics boards were becoming a commodity.

Doing some market research, I identified the market for a multi-purpose TV set-top box that could also surf the Internet. Our VP of engineering and I designed the box and showcased it at CEBIT, a major electronics trade show in Hannover, Germany, to positive reviews. Hewlett Packard's set-top box marketing manager said ours was the most innovative of 31 set-top boxes at the 1998 show. Visiting Beijing, we got orders from Pony TV and another TV maker, but had trouble selling it elsewhere due to our tiny marketing budget.

In an effort to find new business opportunities, I met the VP of marketing at Aureal, a 3D sound design company in Fremont, to discuss emerging audio market trends. While chatting about new audio technologies, the fellow said that MP3 was hot in Germany, where kids were "ripping and burning" music. I had never heard of MP3, which he explained was Layer 3, the sound layer, of the MPEG-1 multimedia technical standard, nor the term "ripping and burning."

"They're ripping music off of CDs and burning them onto hard drives," he said.

"Basically small Walkmans, right?" I asked. "Is anyone selling them in Germany?"

He said MP3 was still a hobby and no vendors had entered the market. The Fraunhofer Institute in Germany, which had developed MP3, sent letters in 1998 to manufacturers saying that they needed to pay license royalties, which stifled the market (http://en.wikipedia.org/wiki/MP3), so nobody had successfully commercialized MP3.

Immediately, I went to Tom and suggested that Genoa sell MP3 players before competitors entered the market, but Tom passed, telling me to focus on set-top box marketing. We had spent six months researching and developing the product so we had too much invested in the new product. I told him the MP3 market would boom since MP3 players were smaller and had more capacity than the Sony Walkman, but he stood firm, so I went back to marketing our set-top box.

To my chagrin six months later, Creative Labs of Singapore, from its development lab nearby, launched the "Rio" player, the first commercial MP3 player, which ignited the market. Within a year, there were dozens of competitors in this fast-growing business, except Genoa. We watched as the MP3 market totally changed the way people listened to music and became the precursor to Apple's iPod player and iTunes service.

Another big miss! Genoa could have invented the first commercial MP3 player! I had the technical teams, but they did not want to create Mosaic at Stanford and now the MP3 player. Being the co-inventor of both technologies would have made my teams famous, they couldn't see making money in the short term from either technology, so they passed – the biggest passes in Silicon Valley history.

When you see an opportunity, jump on it and move fast! Find true believers, build a prototype, and get it in front of customers before competitors. Even if you lose the business race, at least you'll be remembered as one of the innovators. Ideas are a dime a dozen. Fast, brilliant execution is everything!

Cobalt Networks

Breakthrough companies come in all different sizes, shapes and sectors. An inveterate technology watcher, I attended Linux World to look for interesting new technologies and companies that might be pioneers in the next Silicon Valley boom. At the time, I was working at Open Country, which I co-founded with Paul Cubbage, a former Atari marketing manager and the director of Dataquest's software service. Paul wanted to develop a Linux PC, which he thought would undercut Microsoft's stranglehold on the PC market. Looking for an angle to enter the market, we both scoured Linux World in search of new ideas, technologies and partners.

Usually, I look at small booths set up by individual programmers, startups, and small companies since they often have the most innovative ideas and technologies. Indeed, Silicon Valley is filled with closet entrepreneurs with business plans in their back pockets, so it's a delight to search for quirky startups with cool technologies. You never know where you'll find them. After all, I had met Michael Dell, Steven Case, and missed Mosaic, Yahoo! and the MP3 player in the most unexpected circumstances so I knew I would probably meet more amazing entrepreneurs. Seek and ye shall find!

My search was rewarded when I met a small company called Cobalt Networks, which was exhibiting a Blue Cube product that mimicked Apple's translucent blue

Macs and attracted a lot of media attention. I walked over to admire the cube and nodded my approval to one of the salesmen, a young guy in his early twenties, when he said: "That's just eye candy. It's not selling at all. It's just bait for the journalists -- and it works. We're getting a lot of free press."

I chuckled, familiar with the Silicon Valley practice of pre-announcing, but not shipping a product immediately, which is known as "vaporware." As we were chatting, he calmly said: "You know what's really selling? It's not here at the show." I was intrigued. "It's a UL-1 thin server loaded with the Linux OS (operating system) and free software applications for small businesses, which we download free from the Internet. We bundled the solution in the server and it's flying off the racks. The technology guys in companies love it since it gives them ISP-independence (freedom from price gouging by ISPs or Internet Service Providers). If the ISP tries to raise price, they can pull the server from the racks, walk across the street, and get a cheaper deal at a competing ISP. They love the freedom."

I asked the guy if Cobalt needed any investors since strong sales probably meant they were constantly out of cash. He grinned, nodding slowly.

After the show, I immediately called my angel investor and venture capital friends to tell them about Cobalt and its booming sales. All of them yawned, saying that there was no way to make money on open source startups, especially after VA Linux and other Linux companies had crashed in the dot.com collapse. I disagreed, saying Cobalt had bundled the Linux OS and software apps with thin servers into a plug-and-play solution, but still they demurred, even after I told them I had met other famous entrepreneurs like Michael Dell, Steven Case, and been at Stanford at the beginning of the dot.com boom. But they all replied: Forget Linux; it's a money pit.

To my chagrin, or should I say their chagrin, Cobalt Networks was acquired several years later by Sun Microsystems for $2 billion, which would have been a nice return on investment (ROI) for early investors. A $2 million investment for 20% of the company would have netted $400 million in a few years, or $200 million if diluted by half, which would have been one of the biggest ROIs in Silicon Valley history.

However, Sun proceeded to stumble with its Cobalt acquisition, which could have saved it. Instead of using the Linux OS to develop an entire line of low-cost Linux thin servers and rack servers, as HP, IBM, and other competitors did later, it sat on the technology in order to protect its Solaris OS business. Sun saw Cobalt as just a defensive buyout, but that decision turned out to be a fatal mistake. Sun's proprietary server OS strategy was declining in the face of open standards like Linux. Within six years, Sun went out of business while its competitors were thriving with Linux rack server sales. It reminded me of Digital Equipment Corporation (DEC), my Dataquest client in the mid-1980s, who remained with its proprietary minicomputer OS, despite the rise of Sun's low-cost workstations. History repeats itself; the once-innovative fall prey to complacency and the conservativeness of legacy systems and become unwilling to innovate.

Evolve or die! Never remain complacent when you're on top. Some newer, faster, more innovative company is likely to eat your lunch.

MySimon

Innovation is a matter of asking the right questions and acting quickly on them. In early 1998, I got a call from my friend Michael Yang, a Korean entrepreneur who had worked at Samsung America in Silicon Valley, then jumped ship to launch Jazz Multimedia, a chip startup. Like most Silicon Valley startups, Jazz went belly-up and Mike disappeared for a year. I wondered where he went. One day, he came out of hiding and called me.

"In the Korean community, failures don't get a second chance," he said. "But my wife told me to get back to work, so I'm starting another company. I'm calling you to ask you a few questions since you worked for Dataquest. Currently, 10% of the Internet users are women. In five years, what do you think it will be?"

I paused a moment, then answered. "50%. The Internet is going mainstream."

"That's what I think. What will women do on the Internet?" he asked.

"Shop."

"What type of shopping?" I was puzzled, unsure what to reply. "Try asking your wife." I asked my wife and she said "discounts." When I told Mike, he said: "My wife said the same thing. Two women can't be wrong. So I got some programming buddies who work on soft bots to develop an earshot that can compare prices on any product you specify. You just type in a product into my MySimon.com site and the searchbot searches the Internet and lists all the competing prices. Ask your wife what she thinks."

Like any seasoned shopper, my wife was immediately interested and asked for the domain name so she could tell her girlfriends. I told Mike that he was onto something big since she was usually unimpressed with technology. If she fell in love with something, it usually sold well.

Mike went to build MySimon, but rarely updated me on his progress. But one day in 2000, I received a memorable email from him addressed to many of his Silicon Valley friends, which said: "Oh well, guys. We were going to go public but the stock market crash nixed that plan. But I have good news: CNET just acquired us for $700 million.

"Poor Michael," we all groaned. Two years and two months of work and he gets bought out at a humongous price.

If you want to know what sells, ask women. You'll learn faster than just studying business books and attending business conferences. Women account for 80% of consumer purchasing decisions so they wield enormous clout. Since consumers account for 70% of the $15 trillion U.S. market, women decide about $8 *trillion annually in consumer spending. If consumer companies hire more women for top positions, their sales and stock valuations will probably climb. As my daughter often reminds me: Women rock! Heed their wishes and you'll do well in consumer markets.*

2000s: Post-Dot.Com Bust

Raising Venture Capital Overseas

Like everyone else in Silicon Valley, I got caught up in the dot.com boom during the late 1990s and tried launching ventures, but none survived and I couldn't figure out how to survive without salary during the long, risky launch period. Instead of putting all my time into startups, I followed my contrarian instincts and went back to consulting nearly full-time, only helping a few startups on the side. My startup friends kidded me for being "just a consultant", a slap in the face in Silicon Valley where our heroes are startup cowboys and corporate managers. Consultants, usually people out of work and tiding their time until their next corporate job, ranked somewhere between car salesmen and fast-food clerks. I had launched my consultancy in 1989 and survived over a decade during the post-Cold War recession, with no intention of returning to the corporate fold, so I view consulting as a viable, long-term career. My revenues went through the typical roller coaster ride of boom and crash, so I was wary about joining another startup after the dot.crash of 2000 since startups are even more volatile and fail more often.

However, through friends, I met Dr. Antonio Chan of Chanwell Clinics, an associate professor at Stanford Medical School, who wanted to launch an online medical advisory service like Dr. Koop. I was skeptical, but Tony was a warm, amiable fellow who had grown up in Manila, where many of his cardiac patients came from. He had tried raising money from his doctor friends and other angel investors, but was unable to raise a penny. Instead, he said: "Let's go to Hong Kong. I've been introduced to a VC who is interested in investing. I've emailed our business plan so all we have to do is present it."

I had pitched several VCs for previous startups so I knew the drill. Find something you're passionate about, do your homework, find customers, validate your business model, revise your business plan, develop a 10-slide presentation, then be ready to answer a barrage of tough questions.

Tony and I arrived in Hong Kong, where I had given presentations ten years earlier at a multimedia conference, so I felt comfortable in the hustle and bustle of crowded streets, spectacular views and soaring high-rises. Even after its 1997 turnover to China, Hong Kong exuded the freedom and vibrancy of Silicon Valley, which is why it has been so successful economically. When we landed at the airport, my hopes rose.

We found our way to the hotel and were immediately greeted by the VC firm, which took us to a sumptuous dinner overlooking Hong Kong bay. It was everything that one dreams of: a wonderful dinner, gracious hosts, spectacular views and the hope of getting funded. I never enjoyed a Chinese dinner as much as that one in Hong Kong and always recommend my friends to try it once in their lifetime.

The next day we were ushered into the VC's office and sat down in the conference room, nervously preparing our slides. Dr. Chan closed his eyes and repeated his presentation silently, making sure to hit all the key points. The VC walked in and signaled for everyone to be seated. Without delay, Tony introduced our team and launched into his presentation. Before he had spoken five minutes, one of the junior partners leaned over to me and said: "You got your money." I did a double take. Was I hearing him correctly? Tony hadn't even finished his pitch and they wanted to give us money? The fellow nodded and suggested that I tell Tony. I leaned over and whispered to Tony: "We got the money. You can stop."

Tony ignored me and kept presenting. The VC and his partners smiled as I kept trying to stop Tony, but he kept presenting, saying: "I came all this way to present. I can't stop now." We all chuckled. Finally, to make the point, the VC stood up and said: "You have the money. Let's go for lunch." Tony looked disappointed, as if he had come all the way to Hong Kong for nothing. The VC gently smiled and led us to lunch, with Tony looking confused and disappointed after having prepared so much for this presentation.

When an investor gives you money, just shut up and say thanks. Talking too much may give them second thoughts.

To our delight, we raised $5 million in five minutes and were treated to a wonderful Chinese dim sum lunch overlooking Hong Kong Bay. Now that's the joy of life in Silicon Valley, or should I say, Hong Kong. The problem is that our startup ran out of money and closed shop. Another Silicon Valley statistic! But since then, I've co-launched a few more ventures, including helping raise a Series A round for Audience Inc. in Mountain View, California. So you win some; you lose some. The main point is to keep trying and minimize your startup costs.

Don't get extravagant if you raise VC money. It's only fuel for your company at the starting line. Conserve each penny as if it were own, then you'll survive and be able to raise even more money in the future. Even better, don't receive VC money and build your venture with customer prepayments and pure sweat equity.

Startup Failures

Silicon Valley is a "valley of failures" like most competitive regions. Although the media loves to write about Google, Apple, Facebook, SalesForce, Zynga and other high-flying startups, the harsh reality is that most startups fail. Of 1,000 startups launched, probably less than 0.2% receives VC funding, and of those funded about 90% fail, or about 1 out of 5,000 startups enjoy major success. This low success rate is not surprising. Most Hollywood movies fail; most songs fail; most consumer products fail; and most athletic hopefuls fail to make the Olympic team. In all fields, winning is the exception, not the rule. Silicon Valley is no different, just bigger and more global.

Since 1998, I have co-launched half a dozen startups as a serial entrepreneur, usually teaming up with an engineer or programmer and serving as VP of business development. Out of the 15 startups that I seriously considered joining, I helped raise $10 million for 7 startups in open source software, online travel, voice recognition, online health, mobile utilities, panoramic imaging, and networking software for a 47% batting average, which is way above the industry average of 0.2%. But of these 7 funded startups, only one – Audience Inc. of Mountain View, CA – has been able to attract late-stage VC financing. The other survivor is a small, struggling niche player in online travel booking –

or, as investors often say, "the walking dead." Initially, I was disappointed by these poor results but VCs console me by saying: "Par for the course. We lose money on most of our investments too. Keep trying."

Launching and building startups is probably one of the most challenging things I've ever done and I've seen my share of challenges. I've quit many startups because the CEO or team was weak, customers unwilling to pay, or the market saturated. Ideas are a dime a dozen, but building a scalable business is tough, especially in Silicon Valley where dozens of competitors lurk in stealth mode, ready to copy ideas and grab market share from small, unsuspecting startups who naively think they have no competitors. Anything that can go wrong usually does. The few that succeed are well managed as well as lucky. Despite the wonderful weather, energy and resources, the streets of Silicon Valley are not paved with gold, but only filled with endless hard work and unforgiving competitors.

The media loves to trumpet the successful startups – Google, Facebook, Groupon, Zynga, etc. – as though they were a dime a dozen, which inevitably triggers a gold rush of college grads to Silicon Valley every time a hot startup raises money, gets acquired for an enormous sum, or goes public. But insiders know that it's extremely difficult to build a successful venture. Most startups never last more than two years since the odds of succeeding are about as good as winning the lottery.

One always launches a startup with great hope, excitement and enthusiasm, knowing full well the difficulties that lay ahead, but the actual realities of building a business without much money, a brand, customers, or even products or services is daunting – all the while living without a paycheck on one's personal savings. The inevitable problems and setbacks that come daily are daunting beyond belief. It requires incredible mental stamina and perseverance to survive the ongoing difficulties that only seem to grow as the venture grows. Most entrepreneurs quit out of frustration, lack of money or fatigue. They return to the corporate fold to rebuild their bank accounts, spend more time with family and friends, and regain their strength. Many never return to startups, content to collect a regular paycheck, but serial entrepreneurs find the thrill and challenge of startups addictive. Once infected with entrepreneurialism, it's extremely hard to work with startup companies.

What differentiates startup winners from losers? There's no magic formula since each startup differs so much, but VCs and I agree on one thing: the CEO is key. If the CEO thinks only of him/herself, tries to retain all the equity and doesn't listen to others, he/she is likely to fail. Top Silicon Valley engineers, programmers, marketing people and investors look for CEOs who are smart, driven, inspiring, ethical and focused if they're going to take a risk working long years and many years for a startup where the chances for failure are easily 80% or more. They prefer CEOs who "walk the talk", putting their assets and reputations on the line to build their company. First-time CEO successes like Mark Zuckerberg are extremely rare; most startup CEOs fail two or three times or more before they enjoy success.

A smart CEO will hire slowly, selecting only the best, and fire quickly. He/she will set a clear vision and listen carefully to customers, but must be willing to innovate and lead their customers like Steve Jobs did so successfully. They aim ahead of the puck. Top CEOs are like football quarterbacks who have laser focus, but also peripheral vision so they're not blindsided by competitors or rapid market shifts. It's a rare combination of skills that enable CEOs to survive and thrive in the rough-and-tumble, dynamic world of Silicon Valley, where I've seen hundreds of companies go bankrupt in less than six months. Rarely have I met top CEOs with these capabilities. Michael Dell, AOL's Steven Case, and Acer's Stan Shih are some of them. Most startup founders lack the vision, animal energy, drive, focus, leadership qualities and stamina required to lead their companies to market success, so it's no surprise that top startup CEOs are rare. Most VCs can spot weak CEOs within minutes, but finding a Steve Jobs is another matter, like finding a diamond in the rough. When VCs find them, they guard them carefully and employ them as entrepreneurs-in-residence until an opportunity opens up.

If you want to launch a venture, but lack these skills and abilities, don't despair. Even the humblest engineer, programmer or marketer can launch a successful company if you play to your personal strengths and partner with top talent who compensate for your weaknesses. But more important than brilliance is humility, the willingness to listen carefully to one's customers, team members and investors. That's one of Silicon Valley's biggest weaknesses. We have many brilliant people who don't listen and observe well, which is why we fail so often. In the end, markets rule.

If you want to be an entrepreneur, prepare for endless trial-and-error to find your customers and be willing to fail many times. Persistent entrepreneurs eventually find their level of success. For true entrepreneurs, the journey is the reward.

Cisco Over the Edge

Silicon Valley can be a cruel place, not only to startups and employees, but also for major corporations who look invincible. Hard-won fortunes can vanish in months. In early 2000, I was hired as a Cisco contractor to help one of Cisco's business development teams position its Network Navigator software, which allowed Cisco employees, customers and resellers to find software that ran on Cisco router equipment.

In the 1990s, Cisco began an extensive acquisition campaign, buying up all sorts of small networking ventures to fill out its product portfolio. In Silicon Valley, startups are viewed as experiments to test and validate emerging markets. Once they prove their business models, they are often acquired by larger companies at the urging of venture capitalists who want an "exit" to capitalize on their investment. Even after the dot.com crash of 2000, Cisco kept buying startups. Its expanded product portfolio became so confusing that customers could not figure out which Cisco hardware worked with which software. Network Navigator enabled Cisco to grow sales without adding sales people. Cisco asked me if there was a way to position the software to generate even more new revenues.

Immediately, I asked who the target users of the software were. Cisco managers said companies upstream in the supply chain – suppliers of equipment to Cisco – would be the initial test market. But given Cisco's booming sales, I instinctively felt that Cisco could be experiencing double- or triple-ordering, just as I had seen with memory chips in 1984 while working at Dataquest, and that its sales were gliding on thin ice. Other companies were vanishing with the dot.com collapse so I felt it was just a matter of time before Cisco's sales hit a sharp slowdown. Instead of talking with suppliers, I suggested that our team interview customers and their customers, but the managers said: "We'll get to it later."

Unfortunately, we never got there. Six months later, Cisco's sales collapsed and CEO John Chambers had to write off $2.4 billion in excess inventory, one of the biggest write-offs in Silicon Valley history. If my team leaders had listened, we might have saved Cisco a billion dollars by telling Chambers to stop all purchasing immediately. But that's one for the history books now.

Always keep your eyes open for pitfalls and cliffs during a boom. Sometimes, disaster lurks right around the corner.

SalesForce.com

Tripping over opportunities is always a joyful experience.
Often, one never knows which way Silicon Valley will go
or which startups will lead the next industry cycle.
During deep recessions, when there seems to be no light
at the end of the tunnel, East Coast critics love
pummeling Silicon Valley and crowing that it's best days
are over. Schadenfreude delight. They have very short
memories, which I suppose is typical of America's I-
want-it-now mindset. Ever since I was a child, Silicon
Valley has always gone through business cycles, booming
with excess, collapsing from overcapacity, then coming
back bigger and faster – maybe not better – than before.
The 1960s NASA boom, 1980s PC boom, the 1990s
Internet boom, the 2000s dot.com boom, the current
social media, mobile and cloud services boom – always a
new wave of innovation appears out of nowhere just in
time to pull the valley from its cyclical depths of despair.

In 2003, the valley faced another arduous climb out of a
deep, tenacious recession. Again there seemed to be no
hope in sight, only years of more painful cutbacks and
layoffs. Many of my friends and colleagues were
desperate; many left the valley in search of greener fields.

Fortunately, my business partner in Tokyo kept me busy
with consulting projects from major Japanese high-tech
corporations during the downturn. One task was to
explore "utility computing," a techie way of referring to

computing and data management as an online service. The market was picking up since corporate managers were outsourcing their IT work to third-party IT providers like IBM and Hewlett Packard and Indian firms like Tata and Infosys, and companies were seeking ways to cut costs across the board.

One of the utility computing companies I surveyed was SalesForce.com, a tiny, new venture on Market Street in downtown San Francisco. When I walked into the huge, cavernous data center, which had been vacated by a dot.bomb company and was virtually empty except for a few servers, I shook my head in sorrow. The place looked as though a neutron bomb had hit it. Only five engineers were seated around a circular table in one corner of the huge, empty room.

"We provide software as a service, or SaaS," said the CTO. It was the first time I had heard the term. "We want to eliminate all package software and provide services on the Internet."

During the 1980s, I had heard of "net computing," a term popularized by Sun Microsystems, Oracle and other companies that wanted to end Microsoft's packaged software monopoly, but nothing had ever come of the concept. IT managers were unwilling to entrust all of their confidential data to third-party services, so net computers and services remained stillborn. Skeptically, I asked the CTO how many customers that SalesForce.com had managed to sign up.

"Seven thousand, five hundred. But I figure our productivity should be twice as high. My five engineers should be able to support 15,000 customers."

I was stunned. Seventy-five hundred customers for only five engineers! How was that possible? I had never heard of that level of productivity before. Usually, it was several dozen customers per engineer. SalesForce.com was definitely onto something big.

"We provide a turnkey service that makes it easy for sales and marketing teams to keep track of their customers online. Our goal is to serve millions of small businesses. Our business model is scalable since we use a technology platform, standard modules and templates."

I nodded, realizing that they were potentially onto something big. Like Cobalt Networks, which provided low-cost server solutions for small businesses in the late 1990s and sold to Sun for several billion dollars, SalesForce.com was targeting the same sector, which was historically underserved by large technology companies. If they built their business right, they could make a killing and totally redefine the industry.

Although I only spent an hour in the interview, I remember walking out of SalesForce totally amazed and hopeful. Out of the ashes of the dot.com crash emerges another startup that could change the high-tech industry. Instead of outsourcing services to India, SalesForce proposed automating it and keeping it onshore in data centers. The startup had proven its business model in one of the toughest recessions so I knew it had a great future. Little did I know that it would become one of San Francisco's biggest and fast-growing employers in less than five years and a multi-billion-dollar company soon after. As always, my friends asked why I didn't join the company. The reality is that lean, engineering-driven companies with workable business models don't need to hire many sales and marketing people upfront. They can build their businesses organically by making it technically easy to sign up and modify business policies online. In short, I was too early.

Keep your eyes open for hot startups in the wake of market collapses, which favor fast, nimble entrepreneurs who change the rules of the game. Sometimes you're looking at the next Dell, AOL, Google or SalesForce.com. And make sure to follow up later to see if they need your help.

Overlooking Google

Missed opportunities. That could be a major theme of this book since I've seen so many people, including myself, miss big and small business opportunities in Silicon Valley for a variety of reasons: need to pay one's bills, not paying attention, too focused on the past or present, skeptical about new markets and technologies, inability to build a team, fear of risking one's hard-earned savings, family obligations, lack of time, and just plain laziness. "I could have, I should have, I would have." I've heard this excuse and have said it to myself many times. Like Marlon Brando in "On The Waterfront," we all miss big opportunities because we were unwilling to stick out our necks and risk failure in front of family and friends. Even though I've co-launched seven startups, passed on dozens, ended five startups and am launching new startups now, I have often missed big opportunities – AOL, Dell, Skype, Google, Yahoo!, Cobalt Networks, MP3 and YouTube – for a variety of reasons: family illness, no need for my business services, inability to convince my tech partners to build something fast, etc. Most of my Silicon Valley friends have similar stories; it goes with the terrain. You never know where and when you will see the next hot startup. Even VCs miss often and win only 10% of the time.

The irony is that even in Silicon Valley most people rarely innovate because they're too busy or afraid to pursue risky opportunities, even if you describe the opportunity and future in detail as I did with Mosaic, Yahoo! and the MP3 player to my friends, colleagues and investors. Most people are followers, not risk-takers and leaders, including most venture capitalists, which is why Steve Jobs was such a rarity. He didn't listen to "common sense" and innovated in his own way, despite repeated failures. That kind of vision, drive, and resilience is exceedingly rare. Hardcore entrepreneurs like Jobs don't listen to "experts" and investors, but go out and create their own version of the future.

So it was with real disappointment that one of my friends (whose name I'll keep secret to protect the innocent) missed out on one of the greatest startups in Silicon Valley history. When he called me in 2001, he and his wife had both been laid off, not once but several times by startups after the dot.com crash. In 2001, they were ready to leave Silicon Valley and restart elsewhere, but I warned him that it would be a one-way trip out since it would be difficult to return after being out of touch with the industry. Silicon Valley moves too fast for people who are accustomed to a slower, more relaxed pace. I told him to stay put, join another company and hang in there. I'll never forget his desperate words.

"Does Silicon Valley have a future?"

"Yes," I replied. "With the Internet."

"How can you say that? It's a total disaster. Everybody is laying off and going bankrupt."

"We're in the first phase. There will be another wave of innovation."

"Where?"

"I don't know. If I knew, I'd be Bill Gates, but I do know the next boom will be on the Internet."

"What do you think of search technologies?" he asked.

"What about search?"

"Is there a future there?" When I said yes, he responded. "How can you say that? There are 47 search technology companies going bankrupt right now."

"When Michael Dell called me and launched Dell, there were 500 PC computers going bankrupt. It doesn't matter how many companies are going bankrupt, as long as you have a good business model."

My friend asked if I knew of any search technology companies, but I didn't know the field at all and couldn't think of anything. Suddenly, I remembered the gossip I had heard from Stanford colleagues. Even though I had left Stanford in 1994, I kept in touch with the grapevine to keep abreast of the latest trends.

"A Russian guy named Sergey just left Stanford," I replied. "From the math department this time, not the engineering department. He just started a search venture and opened an office in the famous building across the street from the Palo Alto's City Hall where famous startups have been launched."

"What's the company's name?"

"It had a funny name. Goggle. No, Gurgle. No, it sounded like a baby going goo….Google. That's the name! It's based on the math term googol, or 10 to the one hundred power since Sergey is a math whiz."

"Does he do anything different?"

"They do backward attribution."

"What's that?"

"It basically says how many people are citing your webpage, like research papers. The more citations, the better."

"What good is that?"

"I suppose it means your webpage is popular or important."

"Do you know Sergey?"

"No, but just drop by and tell him that I worked at Stanford's electrical engineering department during 1993 and 1994. It's a small circle so he probably knows some of my computer science and engineering friends there."

"Are you sure? Doesn't sound like a very good company to me."

"Look, you don't have a job and I advised my friend Randy Haykin to join Yahoo! as VP of Marketing. He's a venture capitalist now. Maybe Google will be the next Yahoo! After all, they have a funny name and Sergey is a math genius from Russia. Those guys are dangerous."

My friend still seemed unconvinced about Google, but I told him to at least say hi to Sergey since he had nothing to lose. At worst, Sergey might know other companies hiring since Stanford folks always know people creating stuff and starting ventures. It's in the environment.

About four years later, I got a call from my friend, so I asked how Google was doing. There was silence. I asked if Google was struggling and in trouble. Still no reply. I asked if Google was going out of business. Silence, then finally he said:

"I thought you were bullshitting me. I asked all my tech friends and they said Google had nothing new to offer."

"Wait a minute," I interrupted. "Didn't you meet Sergey?"

"No, my buddies said it was a total waste of time." Total silence.

"But you know Russian mathematicians are geniuses. You just missed out on the biggest rocket ride in Silicon Valley history! As the first VP of Marketing, you would have been rich and famous." Total silence, then my friend meekly asked.

"Hey, if you see another Google, let me know."

"If I see another Google, I'm join it myself."

Always walk across the street and kick the tires. You never know what you'll find. It may be the next Yahoo! or Google, or just a bunch of kids going nowhere, but you'll never know unless you investigate.

YouTube

One thing that I'm consistent about is spotting big
opportunities but unable to convince my tech friends to
join me in exploiting them. That's where real
entrepreneurs like Michael Dell, Steve Jobs and Mark
Zuckerberg shine. They're able to motivate and mobilize
the smartest people in town to work together as a team
for no money, often for years. I've seen many
opportunities come along every few years – Dell, AOL,
Mosaic, Yahoo!, Google, MySimon, Cobalt Networks,
Bangalore, and SalesForce.com – so I'm not too upset
about missing one since I know I'll see more. But it's
frustrating not being able to convince tech people to
work with me despite my track record of spotting grand
slam technologies and markets. Easier said than done.
My tech friends often say that I'm too much of a "blue
sky" visionary, even though they know I've seen some of
the biggest startup successes in history. The challenge for
business guys like me is convincing nerds to work with
my startups. Nerds prefer working with nerds. They have
too many career options to give up their dreams and
follow a new, unknown startup, especially one started by
business people, even though some of the biggest
successes in history were started by businessmen like
Steve Jobs, Michael Dell, and Larry Ellison, not
engineers. Most engineers and programmers would
rather the safety of working in a known field with friends
than venture into a totally new field with a "suit."

Unfortunately, most of the grand slam startups in Silicon Valley are found in emerging fields.

In 2005, I had the "joy" of missing another huge opportunity. My friend in Santa Cruz (whose name I'll keep confidential to protect the innocent) told me he had developed a new Web video technology that enabled users to post a video window on any blog or webpage. I asked him for a demo, so we went to a Starbucks. He pulled out his laptop, opened his blog and dropped a video image onto it, but the image wasn't moving.

"Watch," he said, clicking a button. The video started rolling. I jumped with total amazement. The only other time I responded that strongly was when I saw the Mosaic browser for the first time. Both blew me away.

"What are you going to do with it?" I asked with excitement.

"Go to Japan. A CEO wants to use it for Web conferencing so he can update his employees with his latest announcements. Plus, he wants to invest $250,000 into my venture to deploy it."

"Boring," I replied. "And it will take two years for him to invest since Japanese take forever to make decisions. I have a better idea. Why don't we set up a consumer website and let people post videos."

"I don't want to do business-to-consumer (B2C) again. No way to make money."

"But Yahoo! and Google are making money. Maybe we'll be the next Yahoo!"

"Forget it. I'm going to Japan to get the money."

"Just build me a consumer site and I'll promote it. Please!"

My friend shook his head and focused on Japan. I begged him for some tech support for my consumer video idea, but he nixed it and kept flying to Japan to work on the CEO's web conferencing system.

Of course, six months later, my friend emailed: "Guess what, a company just launched a web video site like you said. It's called YouTube.com." My heart sank. Mosaic, Yahoo!, the MP3 player and now YouTube. I had missed another one of the biggest opportunities in Silicon Valley history because my tech friend wouldn't listen to me and build a solution. My batting average was zero, but I consoled myself that at least my intuition was spot on.

I went to the YouTube website, which was OK, and shook my head in despair. Would I always be stuck with missing opportunities? But I jumped up from my seat with a brilliant idea and called him.

"What if we set up a competing Web video site?" I told him. "Maybe we can beat YouTube since it's still early."

"No," replied my friend. "I almost have the money from the CEO."

"Just set me up. I'll market it myself."

But my friend declined and went to flying back and forth to Japan. About eighteen months later, my friend called me.

"Great news! I just raised a $250,000 investment from the CEO. I told you. I was right." Soon after, Google bought YouTube for $1.6 billion. My friend said: "Hey, we could have done that too." A competing startup launched by ex-Microsoft guys whom I had met earlier was acquired for $90 million.

I groaned. "We just missed the rocket ride of the century and you knew that I saw Dell, AOL, Mosaic, Yahoo!, MySimon, Skype, Cobalt Networks, and Google when they were just starting." When will my tech friends ever listen?

Never take no for an answer if you really believe in your vision. Do whatever it takes to get your friends and supporters to build your vision and turn it into reality. Life only rewards doers, not dreamers, talkers or naysayers.

Reviving Japan

Since its spectacular real estate crash in the early 1990s, Japan has muddled along with a series of uninspiring political leaders, poor policymaking, and gun-shy business leaders. Once an Asian powerhouse, Japan has gone to sleep during last two "lost decades." Rarely do you read articles about impressive Japanese entrepreneurs or companies, except for periodic articles about Toyota, Canon, and Sony, but even Sony has missed the bus and is struggling with competition from China and Silicon Valley. The Japan as #1 threat is long gone due to billowing budget deficits, lack of corporate drive and innovation, and an aging society. Will Japan ever revive or is it destined for permanent decline? Will the recent Fukushima earthquake and nuclear plant crisis wake up policymakers and get the country going again?

As an adviser to Japanese companies, I've been following Japan carefully during the past thirty years, providing market research and business strategy plans to major U.S., Japanese, Asian and European organizations doing business in Japan and Asia. Through my business partner in Tokyo, I'm able to monitor the concerns of Japanese government and business leaders behind the headlines: mergers and acquisitions (M&As), promoting entrepreneurialism, broadband services, cloud computing, mobile services, financial services, etc.

Clients like Toyota, Hitachi, NTT, Dai Nippon Printing, Nomura Research, JETRO (Japan External Trade Organization), and METI (Ministry of Economy, Trade and Industry) constantly need to track the latest market trends and emerging technologies and rely on me to update them on Silicon Valley market and technology trends. Occasionally, like Canon, Hitachi and Toyota, they actually listen to my advice and implement some changes and new ventures, but those are the exception, not the rule. In general, Japanese companies are hunkering down due to the long recession and strong yen.

Recently, Japanese companies have been less interested in the U.S. market, focusing their attention on China, Southeast Asia and India. There is palpable concern about the rise of China, which challenges Japan on the economic, political and military fronts. Japan needs the U.S. nuclear umbrella and huge market, but wants its companies to expand their market share in China. As with the United States, it's a delicate balancing act for Japanese government and companies to deal with China. A major challenge is language. Since few Japanese speak fluent English or Chinese, many Chinese fluent in English admit their frustration at being unable to understand Japan.

The gap is not just cultural and language gap. Japan has become increasingly conservative and inward looking. No longer do their young people study abroad nor do companies send their brightest young managers overseas. Even Japanese-speaking foreigners in Tokyo face innumerable obstacles in getting simple services. Historically encumbered by an island mentality, Japan is gradually withdrawing back into its shell.

In order to revitalize its economy, Japan needs to open up to foreigners and involve them more in its economic policies, but it faces a tough climb due to its growing isolationism, strong yen, and rapidly aging population. What can it do to revitalize its stagnant economy? Here are some opportunities:

- Reconstruction: The Fukushima earthquake and tsunami has set back the economy, but reconstruction is already revitalizing the materials, construction and logistics industries. It will take decades to rebuild parts of the Tohoku region devastated by the disaster, which will provide long-term infrastructure jobs. However, like the United States, local procurement practices could slow and raise the cost of reconstruction. Instead of acquiring the best products and services, Japan could end of buying from local companies at much higher cost and added delays. For example, the cleanup robots from the United States were brought in for the nuclear power plant cleanup, despite Japan's leading role in robotics.

- Tap women: Gender discrimination is a major obstacle to an efficient economy. Japan graduates millions of women from universities each year, but the "glass ceiling" and inadequate childcare hinder their careers. If the Japanese government provided more equal hiring and promotion policies and better daycare centers and maternity leave like Scandinavian countries, the Japanese economy would jump a few notches, revivified by their intelligence, experience and drive. Japan is operating with half a brain; it needs to tap the whole mind.

- Tap private savings: Japanese women hold the key to Japan's economy. While the government officials overspent on "bridges to nowhere" to pay off their political buddies in the Liberal Democratic Party (LDP), Japanese women saved. In 2011, The Economist reported that Japanese households held $20 trillion in private savings, an enormous sum of money that is never mentioned in political or economic discussions. What worries Japan's Ministry of Finance is that women, who are trading online, where the ministry currently has little control, mostly control these savings, kept mostly in postal savings accounts. The 20% yen appreciation over the past five years gave Japanese savers $3.5 trillion in increased valuation, which exceeds the $2.4 trillion in Chinese sovereign funds that took over thirty years to amass. Where Japanese women investors decide to invest will have massive influence on global stock markets and the Japanese economy. Politicians and companies cannot afford to ignore these savvy, conservative savers who held onto their savings when global stock markets fell off the cliff in 2009.

- Entrepreneurship: Even though 90% of all Japanese work in small and medium-size businesses, very few try to become entrepreneurs because of the conservative social environment, lack of angel investors and VCs, and harsh bankruptcy laws. The Japanese government is trying to promote entrepreneurship, but they lack the know-how, contacts and savvy as bureaucrats to understand the dynamics and mind of entrepreneurs. Instead of Japanese entrepreneurs working only with other Japanese – or "the blind leading the blind" – they would improve their chances by partnering with experienced Silicon Valley and Asian entrepreneurs.

- Green technologies: Like Germany, Japan leads in environmental technologies because of the government's strict environmental policies since the 1970s. Japan invests over 3% of its GDP in research and development so it is well positioned to sell to China and other fast-growing markets for green buildings, factories and cities.

-   Silver business – Japan's aging population is a huge market for fitness and medical equipment, nutritional products, drugs, leisure travel, senior housing and related businesses. Japanese and foreign companies can turn "lemon into lemonades" by testing and developing "silver" (65-80 years of age) and "gold" (80+ years) products and services, which could then be sold in other countries.

Japan has historically shown the ability to turn disasters into victory so I am confident that it will leverage its wealthy, aging economy into an advanced wisdom economy by marshalling its powerful R&D and private savings. As the saying went during Detroit's decline, if Japan didn't exist, we would have to invent it. Now, Japan needs to reinvent itself, but not alone. The world needs a strong, healthy Japan to offset the economic slowdowns elsewhere.

Whither Silicon Valley?

You've had a chance to hear my stories about Silicon
Valley, about the origins of the valley and some of the
great startup companies and corporate breakthroughs.
It's been one heck of a rocket ride and I'm grateful for
the chance to have been part of Silicon Valley's rise.
Having been in the high tech field for almost 30 years, I
look forward to the next 30 years since I don't plan to
retire – too boring. Instead, I want to work with Silicon
Valley and San Francisco startups that are inventing the
future. Not only are they interesting and challenging,
they create new jobs and industries that are badly
needed.

Does Silicon Valley have a future or will it decline into
industry obsolescence like Pittsburgh and Detroit? Many
journalists and analysts view the rise of China, India and
other emerging nations as a threat to Silicon Valley's
continued dominance in high technologies. They believe
the good times are over. Having grown up in the valley,
I've heard that refrain many times during each recession
and industry challenge – after the Apollo Project reached
the moon, after the 1973 oil shock, after the 1982 oil
price collapse, after the collapse of the Soviet Union,
after the Asian financial meltdown in 1987, after the
dot.bust in 2000, after the 2008 Wall Street bailout, and
now with the rise of China. Frankly, it gets tiring

hearing all these Cassandras lamenting Silicon Valley's fall; so far, they've been proven wrong every time. Silicon Valley is like a gigantic roller coaster capable of bouncing back from failure, with each wave of innovation bigger and faster than the previous ones. It's basically a gigantic learning organization that learns from failure and rebounds quickly, unlike other regions that are stuck with old-fashioned politics, organizations and ways of thinking. Why is this?

Immigration helps tremendously. Since the 1960s, Silicon Valley's population has leapfrogged from a quarter million to over two million today, attracting some of the top tech talent in the world. Although the U.S. government limits H-1 work visas for foreigners, there's movement to get Congress to pass a Startup Visa to retain and attract entrepreneurs, who are the engine of growth for the United States. Chinese and other investors are enrolling their children in U.S. universities and investing into companies under the EB-5 work visa program, which will provide badly needed capital to companies not eligible for VC funding. The United States is still one of the safest investor havens so adventurous investors seeking to ride high-growth industries keep coming to the valley.

Silicon Valley market leaders are growing fast. Intel dominates computer chips. Google and Apple battle for market share in the smart phone business. Online gaming startups like Zynga have triggered a rush of investment. Facebook and Linkedin have triggered hundreds of social media startups in the valley. Cloud computing services offered by Amazon, IBM, HP and startups have passed the "hype stage" and are settling down into a more mature growth phase. Data analytics – a way to analyze the growing flood of Internet and smartphone data – is the latest hot spot. As a Silicon Valley old-timer, I'm always amazed by the speed and size of each successive wave of innovation. Just when people think that Silicon Valley has reached its peak and is entering its decline, it bounces right back with an explosion of new companies and industries.

People ask me: What is the future of Silicon Valley? What they really mean is: Where and how exactly do I make a fortune in Silicon Valley? If I knew, I would be as big and famous as Bill Gates, Steve Jobs or Larry Ellison, but I'm just another Silicon Valley strategist and entrepreneur trying to remain up-to-date and relevant in this fast-moving industry. If I were to place my bets, here's where I see Silicon Valley going during the decade:

Global Diversity - Silicon Valley is a gigantic quilt that has attracted immigrants from hundreds of nations who have turned this region into one of the most open, diverse societies in the world. In our diversity lies our strength. Most Silicon Valley companies look like the United Nations, with each nation and region represented in its workforce. Globalization is accelerating this trend, despite tougher immigration laws on H-1 green cards. Over 100 languages are spoken in some Silicon Valley schools, a trend that will spread throughout the valley. The children of immigrants are graduating from college and entering the workforce in numbers. Fortunately, Silicon Valley has been able to tap the brilliance of its immigrants, which will serve it well in Asia, India, China, Latin America, the Mideast, Africa and other developing regions. As more Indians and Chinese return home to tap into their booming economies, European entrepreneurs from Finland, Sweden, France, Germany, Austria, Spain, Italy, Russia, England, Ireland, Scotland, and Eastern Europe are launching startups and incubators around Silicon Valley and San Francisco. Indeed, the future looks bright as more young, talented immigrants show up on our shores.

Mobile Lifestyles – iPhone and Android applications are booming now and I expect to see millions of more apps being developed over the next few years. Android is growing fast and the new Microsoft-Nokia alliance will challenge Apple and Samsung. App stores will make it easier for mobile users to find what they want, turning the field into a massive mobile retailing battle. Most apps won't sell much, but a few developers and integrators will make a fortune. Apple, Google, Samsung and Nokia are leading the charge into mobile apps and cloud services from their Silicon Valley research labs, which is attracting a host of related companies and new startups. The evolving mobile platforms will be the foundations for the next generation of distributed computing.

Cloud Computing Services – The cloud, or next-generation Internet, will host most consumer and business transactions, content, and interactions since cloud services will be plentiful, varied and cheap or free. Expect to see the rise of billion-dollar cloud ventures and franchises over the next decade, which will make the dot.com boom look small in comparison, since there are more Internet users worldwide who are savvy and constantly seeking new content and services. Cloud services will enable sole entrepreneurs working at home to build international franchises quickly if they pursue the right business strategies. A whole industry of cloud business training and educational services will emerge to help entrepreneurs tap the power of the cloud, which will create tens of millions of jobs for unemployed, underemployed, semi-retired, and even "retired" people seeking to replenish their depleted bank accounts by working into retirement. With baby boomers aging but unable to retire for financial reasons, we will see a boom in cloud businesses that will dwarf previous Internet booms. It will be extremely competitive on a global scale, so smart entrepreneurs will find partners globally to tap local financing and markets. I predict the decade of the 2010s will be the "Era of the Cloud."

Social Media is currently one of the biggest booms because it enables non-technical people to develop new businesses using free or cheap Internet services, tools and applications. The major consumer services like Facebook, Twitter, and LinkedIn make it tough for newcomers to dislodge them, so innovation is shifting beyond platforms to business services and industry sectors, not only in the United States but worldwide. Mobile users will demand easy-to-use apps and services that will be based on smart phones, tablets and other mobile and fixed displays. Indeed, smart phones are the next computing platforms so the battle between Apple, Samsung and Nokia will heat up and create the next wave of social media innovators.

Greentech is a natural for Silicon Valley, especially green-IT, since it leverages our ability to commercialize science and cobble together solutions for intractable problems. Electric cars and batteries, smart solar and wind systems, smart grid, and other alternative energy systems are the wave of the future. However, many of these technologies are heavy infrastructure investments with long-term payback periods, so VCs are focusing on energy conservation technologies with faster payback potential. Longer-term infrastructure will require steady investment by governments and utilities, similar to the role of the Pentagon and NASA in avionics and electronics.

Preventive Healthcare – Self-care, personalized medicine or health 2.0 will be the next boom in healthcare innovation in Silicon Valley because of tech-savvy aging baby boomers seeking greater control over their health and lives. Anti-obesity campaigns will stimulate innovation in nutrition, mobile applications and personalized health services that are part of our future self-care systems. Silicon Valley is attracting almost half of VC funding in life sciences because of the presence of Stanford and UC San Francisco's "BioCity", which is shaping up as the new "Bio Corridor." To the east, UC Davis is also attracting agricultural and biomedical companies and startups.

Agrotech is emerging rapidly as a potential solution to the problem of global warming, water shortages, skyrocketing food prices, and desertification. By growing smarter and more efficiently, Silicon Valley and UC Davis technologists can help growers to develop better, faster, and cheaper ways to get their food to market or for communities to grow their own food.

Indeed, there are so many emerging markets, technologies and business models, both in the United States and globally, that there is no shortage of opportunities for savvy Silicon Valley entrepreneurs who are increasingly global in reach. As Alan Kay fondly said: "The best way to predict the future is to invent it."

Thus, the future of Silicon Valley will be no different than the past, just bigger, faster, and more global. Silicon Valley is no longer just a place; it has become a state of mind, a spirit, and a way of thinking, living and creating that can be pursued anywhere. As long as the entrepreneurial fire exists, Silicon Valleys will exist in different forms around the world. Perhaps that is Silicon Valley's ultimate contribution to the world -- not just the many technologies and companies that we've created and built, but our ability to give vision and hope to billions of people around the world who want better lives and to collaborate with them so they can create real value and companies from very little. If that is our ultimate contribution, then I will always be proud to say that I'm from Silicon Valley and I'm here to collaborate and partner with you to create our common future, for we are part of one world, one community living on a tiny sphere floating in the vast cosmos.

San Francisco, California

June 2012

Sheridan Tatsuno, Principal, <u>Dreamscape Global</u>

Sheridan Tatsuno is principal of Dreamscape Global, a high-tech market research and strategy company in San Francisco. Since 1982, he has advised over 700 high-tech companies in the U.S., Japan, Asia and Europe while working as a senior analyst at leading market researcher Dataquest/Gartner Group (1982-1989) and Dreamscape Global (1989-present). A visionary thinker, Silicon Valley business strategist, and thought leader, Mr. Tatsuno was involved with the early stages of the "Intel Inside" marketing campaign, Nokia's global strategy planning, AMD's breakthrough sub-$1000 PC, and Canon's networked equipment strategy. His strength is helping companies develop breakthrough strategies.

Mr. Tatsuno has written two business books on Japan: "The Technopolis Strategy" and "Created in Japan," which were optioned for television, respectively, by Central Independent Television plc of London for Japan Dreaming (1991) and Alvin Perlmutter Inc. of New York for The Creative Spirit 4-hour PBS series (1992). Since 1991, he has written 14 screenplays and preparing four more.

Mr. Tatsuno has studied in France and Germany, worked in Caracas, Venezuela and Japan, and traveled on business to Japan, Asia and Europe. He speaks and reads Japanese, Spanish and French. His current activities can be found at www.ryze.com/go/tatsuno,

www.facebook.com/sheridan.tatsuno?ref=tn_tnmn

Contact: info@dreamscapeglobal, 415-254-4195

www.ingramcontent.com/pod-product-compliance
Lightning Source LLC
Chambersburg PA
CBHW072024190526
45166CB00015B/383